Dedication

To Vicki for encouraging me
and assisting in the major
reorganisation of our home
with its countless possessions,
resulting in calmness and
sanity. It was a lot of work but
eventually very rewarding.

Imprint

A FIREFLY BOOK

Published by Firefly Books Ltd. 2007

Copyright © 2007 Conran Octopus Ltd.

First printing

Published in the United States by
Firefly Books (U.S.) Inc.
P.O. Box 1338, Ellicott Station
Buffalo, New York 14205

Published in Canada by
Firefly Books Ltd.
66 Leek Crescent
Richmond Hill, Ontario L4B 1H1

Published in 2006 in the United Kingdom by
Conran Octopus Limited,
a part of the Octopus Publishing Group
2–4 Heron Quays, London E14 4JP
www.conran-octopus.co.uk

Consultant Editor Elizabeth Wilhide
Publishing Director Lorraine Dickey
Editors Sybella Marlow and Zia Mattocks
Art Direction & Design Jonathan Christie
Color illustrations Robin Chevalier
Picture Researcher Liz Boyd
Production Controller Jane Rogers

Printed in China

Publisher Cataloging-in-Publication Data (U.S.)
Conran, Terence.
   How to live in small spaces : design,
furnishing, decoration, detail for the smaller
home / Terence Conran.
[224] p. : col. photos. ; cm.
Includes index.
Summary: Guide to making the best of small
space living: from decoration and furnishing to
design and detail, from spatial alterations to
retailers and suppliers.
ISBN-13: 978-1-55407-242-2
ISBN-10: 1-55407-242-5
1. Room layout (Dwellings). 2. Interior
decoration. 3. Space
(Architecture). I. Title.
747 dc22   NK2115.C66 2007

Library and Archives Canada Cataloguing in
Publication
Conran, Terence
   How to live in small spaces : design,
furnishing, decorations,detail for the smaller
home / Terence Conran.
Includes index.
ISBN 1-55407-242-5
1. Small rooms–Decoration. 2. Small houses–
Decoration. 3. Room layout (Dwellings).
4. Interior decoration. I. Title.
NK2117.S59C65 2007   747.'1
C2006-905329-4

TERENCE CONRAN
HOW TO LIVE IN SMALL SPACES

DESIGN | FURNISHING | DECORATION | DETAIL FOR THE SMALLER HOME

FIREFLY BOOKS

Contents

Area by Area

Case Studies

Introduction

Previous pages The Micro-Compact Home (M-CH) by Richard Horden, Lydia Haack and John Hoepfner is only 485 sq. ft. (46 m²) square. Conceived as a low-cost housing solution, each unit can be stacked and includes a kitchen, work/dining area, two beds and a bathroom on three interlocking levels.

1 Small space living means making the most of whatever you have – even if it is below ground, like this sunken work area neatly lined with shelving. **2** A newly built house on a narrow infill site is one room wide and six stories high. Floor-to-ceiling windows create a sense of openness.

Size, as they say, is not everything. If many of us are living in homes smaller than those in which we grew up, it is not necessarily because circumstances (economic ones, in particular) have forced us to. A recent statistic widely published in the British press reveals that half the households in two of London's more prosperous boroughs, Westminster, and Kensington and Chelsea, are single households, and presumably quite a substantial proportion of these are apartments. As has long been the case in New York, Tokyo and Hong Kong, it seems clear that people are increasingly prepared to make the best of small space living for the sake of a good location. A desire to live near to one's place of work and to avoid long commutes plays a significant part in decisions about where to live.

It used to be the case that one's advance up the property ladder could be charted in terms of increasing floor area, as the student bachelor apartment roughly the size of a broom closet was exchanged for the unimaginable luxury of a one-bedroom apartment, which, in turn, eventually led to a family house with several bedrooms and a family-sized yard. This ever-expanding progression is not quite as inevitable today as it once was. The premium price that space commands, particularly in urban areas and densely populated parts of the globe, increasingly means that sooner or later many homeowners (and renters, too, for that matter) find themselves having to rethink their spatial requirements and "downsize" their expectations accordingly.

Probably the smallest home I have ever lived in was a single rented room measuring about 10 x 12 ft. (3 x 3.7 m) on the top floor of a house in Warwick Gardens – actually, it was the first place I lived in when I came to London. As an ambitious young designer, I wasted no time putting my own stamp on my surroundings with bright color, Paolozzi prints and furniture I had designed and made out of welded metal and rope. In the room across from mine lived a woman named Olive Sullivan, who was at that time decorating editor of *House & Garden* magazine. Occasionally I would get a glimpse into her room, which, much to my amusement, was smothered in patterns largely featuring, as I recall, rosebuds.

2

1

2

Each of the 342 rooms has the same basic grid and parameters, but what eventually emerged were very different interpretations of what a hotel room should be

They were two very similar rooms in size, scale and proportion, but approached in two very different ways, to say the least. I suppose the point I am trying to make is that size need not inhibit personal expression: you can make a small place just as much your own as you can a larger one.

A similar point can be illustrated by Madrid's Hotel Puerta America, a "designer" hotel with a difference. Each of its 12 floors is the work of a different architect or designer – those involved on the project included Norman Foster, Ron Arad, Marc Newson and Arata Isozaki. A stipulation of the brief was that the different architects and designers involved were asked not to talk to each other. Each of the 342 rooms has the same basic grid and parameters, but what eventually emerged were very different interpretations of what a hotel room should be.

Whether small space living has been forced upon you or is something you have chosen more positively, this book is for you. It is a "house book" in the fullest sense, in that it covers just about every aspect we could think of, from decorating and furnishing to design and detail, from spatial alterations to distributors and suppliers. Tailoring a small space to meet your needs, and meet them well, is not a question of superficial styling or purely decoration; it is a design job. Throughout, we have firmly stressed the practicalities of how to make a small space work better and feel larger: I always say that if you get the bones right – the basics of structure, function and layout – the rest is relatively easy. You may well require professional assistance to translate your ideas into reality, but you need the ideas in the first place, and I hope this book will provide you with more than a few.

Space is such a luxury these days, and widely perceived as such, that many people cannot help but feel cheated or hard done by if their homes are not as spacious as they would have liked. This is one of the first attitudes that you must overcome if you are going to enjoy small space living to its fullest. Small homes do entail some degree of compromise, but it is not all about sacrifice. There are many positive aspects to the situation, and it is well worth it to remind yourself of them.

3

4

5

1 All-white decor accentuates the precise outfitting of this multipurpose space.
2 "Optibo" is a prototype apartment designed by Bo Larsson. A touch screen just inside the foyer furnishes the space on command. A banquette, chairs, dining table and double bed are all stored away in a compartment 2 ft. (0.6 m) deep under the cherrywood floor. Touch one of the icons and the piece you have selected rises up from the floor on a hydraulic lift.

Here is a brief list:

■ Opting for a smaller home may enable you to live in a location that you might otherwise not be able to afford, closer to where you work, for example, or within walking or cycling distance of a city center.

■ Smaller homes are cheaper to run, in just about every respect, but notably in terms of fuel bills, utilities and taxes.

■ When it comes to choosing materials – flooring, for example – you will be able to afford those of a better quality because the surface area that you will need to cover will be limited. The same applies to details such as switches and handles – you will need fewer, so you can afford better.

■ Small spaces, indoors and out, are easier to maintain. Clearing up or cleaning the house will no longer be a task that no sooner completed must be started all over again. The time you save on routine chores can be spent doing something you really enjoy.

■ Small space living forces you to be selective in your purchases, and this is no bad thing at a time when choice can be overwhelming and many people own and acquire much more than they use or need.

■ The tight planning that small spaces demand often makes everyday tasks easier to perform – think of the economy of movement and control you gain by working in a small, well-planned kitchen.

You may well think of other advantages that you could add to the list. At any rate, it seems to me that the pros potentially outweigh the cons, and certainly provide compelling enough reasons to make the most of whatever space you have. Perhaps most persuasive, however, is the fact that living in a small space forces you to think laterally and creatively and not be bound by convention. Instead of allocating specific functions to separate rooms, you will inevitably need to consider the space as a whole, linking or grouping activities together without the conventional boundaries of walls, as well as building in as much as you can behind the scenes. At their best, small spaces can be both inclusive and flexible, which is perfectly in tune with the relaxed and informal way we want to live now and will no doubt continue to want to live in the future.

At their best, small spaces can be both inclusive and flexible, which is perfectly in tune with the relaxed and informal way we want to live now

1

2

1 Hanse Colani Rotor House, designed by Luigi Colani, contains a 65 sq. ft. (6 m²) cylinder that encloses a bedroom, kitchen and bathroom. The remotely controlled cylinder rotates left or right in the main living room to enable you to access whichever room you want.
2 Sheds, shacks and other outbuildings can provide useful inspiration for small space living. Living with the minimum is a challenge, but it can be very liberating.

3 Tree tents by Dutch artist Dre Wapenaar were originally designed for the Road Alert Group in Britain, a group of activists who fight against road construction by setting up temporary residence in trees to prevent them from being cut down. Subsequently, a campsite bought the tents and they are rented out for five months of the year. Two adults and two children can sleep on the main floor, which is about 9 ft. (2.7 m) in diameter.

4 Space Box student housing at Utrecht University in the Netherlands. These stacked modules provide an intriguing solution to student housing at a time when there is an acute shortage of accommodation on many campuses.

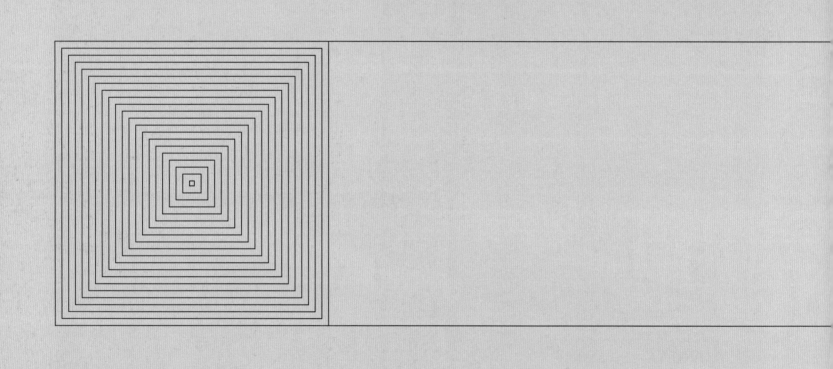

PART 1

MAKING THE MOST
OF SMALL SPACES

DESIGN & PLANNING

Living in Small Spaces

When you do not have much room at your disposal, every square foot has to earn its keep. Thinking laterally, both in terms of spatial planning and in adjustments to your lifestyle, can be highly effective.

In fundamental terms, all homes, of whatever size, type or character, must satisfy a number of basic needs. If you are at a stage of life when most of what you do every day – working, eating and socializing – happens away from home, you still need a place to sleep, to enjoy a little privacy and to recharge your batteries. Even if you travel light through life, accumulating few possessions, these still need to be kept somewhere. And there are other essentials that every home should provide, namely somewhere to relax, a bathroom and a kitchen area, however compact and minimal. In fact, this is what most good hotel rooms provide in capsule form.

Most of us, of course, do not have such streamlined existences. The interests and activities we pursue, as well as our individual preferences, make their own spatial demands. When your home is on the small side, however, you have to accept that something has to give. Spending some time assessing your requirements and thinking about what is optional and what is truly necessary can help point you in the right direction.

1

■ Do you like to entertain at home? Is it important to you to be able to have friends over for dinner, or to have family to stay?

■ Do you frequently have people staying with you overnight or for extended periods?

■ Are you a keen cook, or do you eat out often and the rest of the time heat up something in the microwave?

■ How much food do you keep on hand on a regular basis? Do you shop weekly at a supermarket for bulk supplies or simply pick up whatever you need whenever you need it?

■ Do you prefer baths or showers? Is it absolutely essential that your bathroom include a tub or would a good, powerful shower be more than adequate?

■ Do you work from home on a regular basis? Do you need a dedicated work area or simply somewhere to plug in your laptop?

■ Would you like access to outdoor space? Do you enjoy gardening or simply require a sheltered spot to sit outdoors in warm weather?

■ Think about what you own. Do you buy and accumulate a lot of books? CDs? Clothes? Could you part with some of your belongings to ease pressure on storage space?

■ How suitable is your furniture for small space living? Would flexible, multipurpose designs work better?

■ Think about the future. How long do you expect to live in your present home? What changes in lifestyle can you anticipate during that time?

1 This tiny Parisian studio has been decorated in pure white to enhance the sense of space. The glossy floor and gleaming metallic open staircase help spread the light around. On the loft level is a sleeping platform, a freestanding bathtub and a sink built into an open storage unit.

Levels of change

Living happily in small spaces often necessitates change. The first level of change costs nothing and simply requires an adjustment of your expectations. The process of self-assessment should begin to throw out some ideas as to how you can best accommodate your needs within the space at your disposal. While it is important to be realistic – a grand piano is not going to fit comfortably in a tiny basement apartment, even if you could sit at it – it is also crucial to recognize your own priorities and not be swayed by others' expectations of what a home should provide. Suit yourself. If a large bathroom with an adjoining dressing area would give you more satisfaction on a daily basis than a lavish kitchen, let that consideration inform your decisions. Similarly, getting rid of redundant belongings may cause a little emotional upheaval, but if that is all it takes to provide a comfortable fit, the process is well worth it.

The second level of change comprises various strategies that are essentially superficial, but can have far-ranging consequences in the way you experience your home. Decorating your home to make the most of light and air, simplifying architectural details, replanning routes, building in storage and investing in furniture and fixtures that make the most of space require some financial outlay and a little extra effort, but all have the potential to make your home feel more spacious, work more efficiently and probably increase in value.

The third level of change entails altering the structure of your home in a more radical fashion, either to improve the way different areas work or to add extra space by converting redundant areas such as attics and basements, or by building on an addition. If you anticipate staying in your home for a number of years and your budget permits, making this type of change represents a sensible investment of time, effort and money.

1 Open-concept layouts are naturally more spacious. Here, the upper level is only minimally screened with railings, while the absence of doors on the level below allows natural light through to the separate areas. The stairs have see-through treads.
2 Small spaces do not come much smaller. This tiny London apartment features a home office, sleeping platform and clothes storage in one compact space. Increasingly, many people are prepared to live in smaller homes for the sake of a good central location.

Don't be swayed by others' expectations of what a home should provide – suit yourself

Reassess your priorities

Level 1

■ Shed excess baggage. Sort through your possessions and discard what you don't need, don't wear and don't use.

■ Take a long hard look at your present lifestyle and allocate space accordingly.

■ Be realistic about what you can fit in. Very large pieces of furniture, particularly those that serve only one function, devour space unnecessarily.

Level 2

■ Adopt decoration strategies that are naturally space-enhancing, such as choosing light colors and keeping backgrounds neutral. Opt for materials that are similar in tone throughout the space.

■ Mirrors and reflective surfaces make the most of available natural light and help make the space seem larger.

■ Pay particular attention to artificial lighting. Well-placed lighting has a vast impact on our impression of space.

■ Simplify architectural detail to reduce visual clutter.

■ Build in as much storage space as you can.

■ Choose furniture that is adaptable, flexible and multipurpose.

■ Replan circulation areas so that you use all the space at your disposal.

■ Group activities within multipurpose layouts rather than segregating different functions unnecessarily.

Level 3

■ Open up your home internally – knock down nonload bearing walls or create new openings – or create new exterior openings.

■ Convert underused areas in attics and basements.

■ Add on to your home sideways, upward, outward or even downward to provide additional room.

■ Convert a garage, shed or outbuilding to provide extra accommodation.

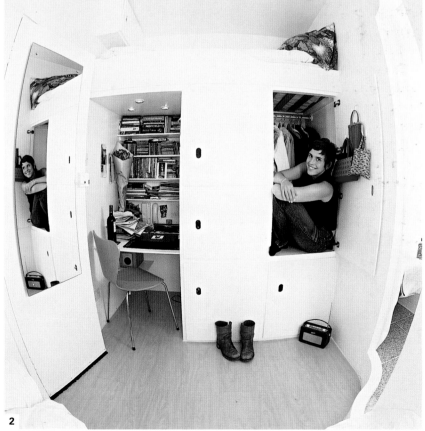

2

Living in Small Spaces

1

1 Careful planning allows you to address storage needs in a thorough way early on in the design process, so that you can allocate sufficient space for all your possessions. Here, a shelving unit serves as a room divider, screening a living area from the kitchen.

Looking for potential

Whatever strategy you adopt, your plans will be grounded in reality only if you know your home inside out. A vague impression will not do. You need to study different areas in detail, measure as accurately as you can and get it all down on paper so that you can consider the possibilities objectively.

Homes that are more generous in size have built-in tolerance – or room to maneuver. When you are living in a small space, a matter of a few inches can make all the difference, particularly when it comes to planning areas such as kitchens and bathrooms.

How to make a plan

■ A fitted approach tends to be the most practical choice for small spaces, not merely for kitchens and bathrooms, but for other areas in the home. When you are designing built-in spaces – or hiring someone else to do the work – you need to be particularly accurate. It is not simply a question of fit, though that is obviously important. The most successful built-in spaces are those that are fully integrated within the framework of the room and that, too, calls for precision.

■ Equip yourself with graph paper, pencil, ruler and a measuring tape. Don't use a cloth tape – they stretch. Electronic measures, often used by real estate agents to measure properties, are not entirely reliable. Steel tapes and rules are the best.

■ Measure each area or room in your home. Get a friend to help you hold the tape straight.

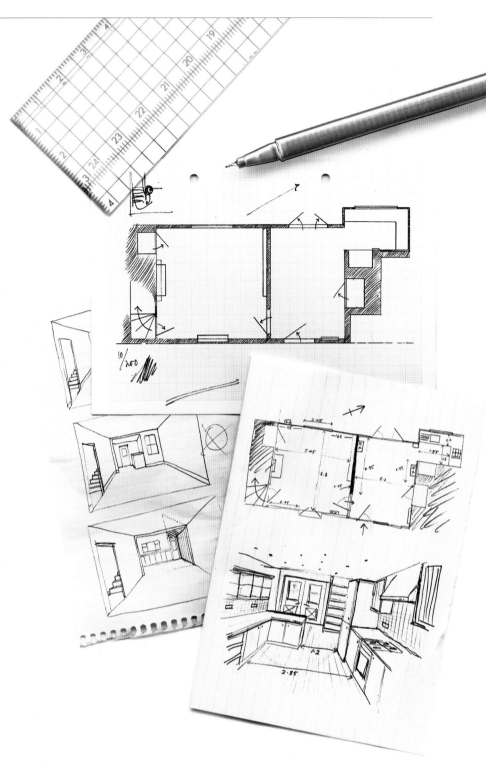

Mark down the measurements on a rough sketch of the area in question.

■ Measure and note the position of features such as vents, fireplaces, alcoves, windows, doors, closets and other principal details. Note the position and number of power outlets and light switches. Note in which direction doors and windows open.

■ Working to scale, draw up a plan of each room or area on graph paper using a steel rule and a sharp, hard pencil. A useful scale for general living areas and bedrooms is roughly 1:50, where ¼ in. represents 1 ft. (or 2 cm represents 1 m). For smaller areas such as kitchens and bathrooms, it is often more practical to work at a scale of 1:20 so that you include enough detail.

■ Once you have drawn up the basic dimensions, mark on all the features that you have previously measured and noted on your sketch plan.

■ Other aspects to note include basic orientation. Does the room receive morning sun or sun later in the day? You should also mark down any surfaces or features that require repair or show signs of damage from cracking or moisture.

■ To visualize alternative layouts or to experiment with furniture placement, draw the shapes of appliances or pieces of furniture to the same scale on a separate piece of paper, cut them out and move them around on your scale plan until you determine the optimal

arrangement.

■ For rooms with fixed cabinetry, such as kitchens and bathrooms, drawing up elevations – or plans of the walls seen face on – can also be very useful.

Storage

Small space living tends to bring storage considerations to the forefront. People who live in larger houses often have storage problems, too, but it is fair to say that they are generally able to ignore the issue for longer – until every nook and cranny has been filled up. When your home is a tight squeeze to begin with, storage must be carefully thought out right from the start. When every square foot of your home counts, the last thing you want to do is use valuable space to house redundant clutter.

How to get rid of things

You have bought your first condo or loft – or you have sold the family home and you are downsizing. The movers have shifted the last crate out of the van and now you are sitting in your new home surrounded by boxes, wondering how you are ever going to accommodate it all.

Moving day is a little late to be having such thoughts. Before you even begin to pack the first box with your belongings, you should instigate a thorough assessment and clear-out, so that everything you move into your new home (and what, after all, you are paying to have moved) are all things that you really want and need.

Be as ruthless as you dare. Most of us accumulate more belongings than we can ever use or even look after properly. Dejunking is often a more productive process when it is jointly undertaken. Enlist the help of a friend or family member who will not share your emotional attachments to the things you own and who can help keep you in a more objective (and critical) state of mind.

■ Start by eliminating whole categories of possessions. If you are moving to a place without a yard or to one where the yard requires minimal upkeep, you can ditch most, if not all, of your gardening tools and accessories (along with their accompanying manuals). If you are hanging on to equipment or sports gear long after your enthusiasm for the pursuit has waned, take the opportunity to get rid of it.
■ Give yourself a fresh start by shedding past baggage. Separate treasured mementos from the paper trail that documents the previous years of your life and career in unnecessary detail.

■ Get rid of anything you don't like – clothing that has never suited you, books that you will never read, gifts that do not appeal to your taste (it's the thought that counts).
■ Throw out anything that is broken, damaged, beyond repair or in any other sense no longer usable.
■ Get rid of duplicates. You do not need two sets of dishes and glassware, one for best and one for everyday. One decent all-purpose set will do.
■ Pare down the contents of your wardrobe, as well as your collections of books, CDs, DVDs and videos, to a manageable size.
■ Keep the things you love.

Storage

1 Ingenious built-in storage for books features thin shelves set within a metal framework. With the books arranged on their sides, the effect is of unsupported stacks. The shelving is neatly integrated into a hallway.
2 Built-in storage makes sense in small kitchens, in particular, and helps integrate different service points. Here, a slight variation on the theme of wall units positions cabinets slightly apart from one another, so that the effect is less dominant.
3 Built-in storage demands a wholehearted approach. This doorway is framed with sleek wooden cupboards that extend to one side to form a low plinth that incorporates more storage space.
4 Areas high up the wall can be usefully devoted to storage, provided there is some ready means of access, such as this library ladder on casters.

5 Illustrations show different solutions for alcoves on each side of a chimney breast (clockwise from top left): freestanding storage furniture; floor-to-ceiling shelving; floor-to-ceiling cupboards; shelving over closed cupboards.

Planning built-in storage

Built-in storage is generally a better solution for small space living than relying on freestanding pieces of storage furniture. While it is true that you may have to sacrifice a little floor area, the effect is less intrusive visually. A wall of built-in cabinets hidden behind flush panels can house a vast amount of possessions and still look like a wall. If you were to store the same possessions in freestanding armoires, chests of drawers and bookcases, the room would feel much more cramped and claustrophobic. Added to which, freestanding storage pieces, unless positioned snugly within alcoves, tend to result in awkward and unusable margins of floor area on either side.

Built-in storage works particularly well in areas that feature fixed plumbing and other service points, such as kitchens and bathrooms. Not only is the overall effect more integrated and seamless, but building in fixtures such as toilets and sinks also allows you to exploit the spaces behind the panels as storage areas.

■ Plan built-in storage in conjunction with your scale drawings. Consider your storage needs overall and think how you might accommodate these throughout your home, rather than adopting a piecemeal, room-by-room solution. Hallways and other "neutral" areas, for example, are great places for built-in cabinetry, which can hold a wide range of belongings, from outdoor clothing to vacuum cleaners and books to spare bedding.

■ Consult catalogs and manufacturers' brochures to get an idea of common dimensions of prefab shelving units and cupboards. Measure what you intend to store and allow a generous margin for future expansion.

■ Adopt a wholehearted approach whenever possible. Shelve an entire wall from floor to ceiling or fill an entire wall with built-in cabinets.

■ Pay attention to scale and proportion. Low-level cabinets or shelving running around the perimeter of the room provide a horizontal emphasis that works well in modern interiors. Many period homes feature alcoves flanking the chimney breast: these are best treated the same way.

■ To keep the effect reticent, outfit cabinets with doors that can be painted to match the wall. Alternatively, doors, panels and drawer fronts made of semi-transparent material add to the sense of spaciousness.

■ Consider accessibility. High-level shelving or cabinets will need to be reached by a ladder of some sort. Doors must open the right way and not obscure traffic routes. If space is very tight, think about using sliding or accordion panels.

■ Think laterally. Storage can be built into many different locations – under window seats, within stair treads and under floors.

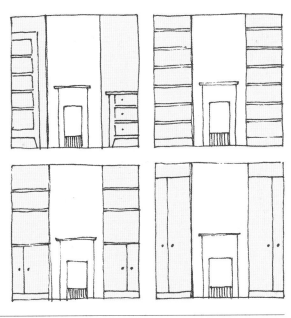

5

1 The entire gable-end wall has been taken over by a combination of storage and display. The red background and red ladder allow the collection to be seen as a whole.
2 When planning built-in storage, it is important to tailor the dimensions of cabinets and drawers to what is being stored – narrow shelves for small items, deep cabinets for hanging space.
3 There are many different accessories available for customizing the interiors of cabinets and drawers. These wooden posts attached to the base of a kitchen drawer help keep stacks of dishes separate from one another to prevent them from sliding, chipping or breaking when the drawer is opened and closed.

Customizing built-in storage

In terms of storage, there is no such thing as one-size-fits-all. All types of built-in storage, from kitchen and bathroom cabinets to shelves and cupboards, need to be adapted to some degree to suit the sizes and shapes of the various things you will be storing in them. Customization has several very important practical roles to play. It ensures objects can be located and retrieved without difficulty, it keeps them in good condition and it makes the fullest use of available storage space. At the same time, customization can also be a way of adding style and value to your storage arrangements by upgrading door and drawer fronts, for example, or opting for high-quality catches and handles.

Width and depth

Shelving, either on its own or within cupboards and built-in cabinetry, needs to be spaced according to the height and width of what you are storing there.

■ Adjustable shelving within kitchen and bathroom cabinets allows you to arrange your storage space to suit what you regularly buy and consume. Many shelving systems designed specifically for books are also adjustable – though in my experience they rarely are readjusted once they have been set up. However, such systems do at least allow you to be flexible at the outset. It causes far less grief to move a shelf up a fraction to accommodate those large-format books you had not taken into account than it does to call the carpenter back to remake the shelving unit that was just installed.

■ Narrow shelves are good for glassware, medicine bottles, bathroom accessories and small containers and jars. If you keep your entire collection of herbs and spices on a single deep shelf, for example, jars and bottles will get pushed to the back and overlooked. Glasses kept on narrow shelves are easy to access with less risk of chipping.

1

The backs of closet or cabinet doors can be exploited as storage areas, especially for items that are not particularly bulky

Inserts

A wide range of accessories are available to allow you to adapt closet and drawer interiors so that they can be used to their fullest extent. Alternatively, you can always improvise, using your own boxes, jars or other containers.

■ Drawer dividers are a good idea for knives and cutlery (flatware) or for separating small accessories or items of clothing, such as socks and scarves.

■ Some kitchen manufacturers produce special inserts designed for bottles that are stored upright.

■ Lined wicker baskets, lidded boxes and other containers can be used to store like with like within a drawer, built-in shelves or closet.

Racks and rails

The backs of closet or cabinet doors can be exploited as storage areas, especially for items that are not particularly bulky.

■ Install racks and rails on the back of your closet door to hold ties and belts.

■ Canvas shoe tidies can similarly be suspended from the back of closet doors.

■ Hang up brushes, brooms and other cleaning tools on the back of broom-closet or utility-room doors.

Style

You can give existing storage units a makeover by upgrading facing materials, handles and hardware.

■ Choose better-quality materials for doors, panels and drawer fronts. Some companies specialize in replacement doors for standard kitchen and bathroom cabinets. Alternatively, you could purchase custom-made doors and drawer fronts from a carpenter, specifying the material you want.

■ Upgrade catches and handles. Details make a great deal of difference, especially in small spaces, where they are harder to ignore. For a relatively small price, you can give your home a real feeling of quality.

Scale & Proportion

The two most common ways of defining small spaces are in terms of the number of rooms ("a one-bedroom apartment") or in total floor area ("a 320 sq. ft./30 m^2 bachelor"). Neither gives the full picture. The way we experience space is not strictly quantifiable, but arises out of less tangible elements, which one might summarize as the way the space feels. There are many ways of enhancing the feeling of spaciousness. Some of these may even result in a direct loss of floor area. Often what makes a home truly liveable does not boil down to one or two extra square feet here or there, but an overall spatial quality that literally gives you room to breathe. A small space that is well proportioned will inevitably be more comfortable and accommodating than one that is awkwardly shaped and poorly scaled. Three main elements come into play here: architectural detail; views and sightlines through openings such as windows and doors; and reflections and volume.

1 Architectural detail does not necessarily have to mean period features. This glass-floored landing, which allows light through to the level below, provides great visual interest and a sense of drama.

Architectural Detail

"Period features," a term loved by real estate agents when advertising homes with character, can be a mixed blessing in small spaces. Not all architectural detailing is historic, of course, but it is fair to say that contemporary spaces tend to be more self-effacing when it comes to such decorative embellishments and flourishes as cornicing and architraves. Fireplaces, or rather the framework that surrounds them, are architectural details of a more imposing nature.

If your home forms part or all of an older property, it may include some of the following features:

- Central ceiling rosettes, generally made of plaster. Georgian and Edwardian examples can be relatively refined; Victorian versions are typically more elaborate, even flowery.
- Cornicing running around the top of the walls, just below the ceiling. Again, styles vary from the elegant egg-and-dart designs of the Georgians to more elaborate Victorian examples.
- Picture rails set below the cornicing.
- Dado (chair) rails about one-third of the way up the wall.
- Dado (wainscot) panels covering the portion of the wall below the dado rail.
- Baseboards, which may be particularly high in an older property.
- Wooden moldings and architraves surrounding doors and windows.
- Fireplace surrounds.

It is generally believed that ripping out period features such as the detailing listed here amounts to architectural vandalism. If your home has particular architectural or historic character, you would be well advised to keep it as intact as possible. However, not all "period features" are worthy of loving conservation. Over the years, many become clogged and obscured with successive layers of paint, or suffer chipping and cracking and other forms of damage. If your home is a loft or apartment that forms part of a conversion of a larger property, those details that remain may serve only to call attention to the fact that rooms have been partitioned, for example, to make separate entrances or access points. If this is the case, and the detailing is of no great distinction or has already been mutilated, it may be preferable to remove some or all of it completely.

Scale & Proportion

Minimizing architectural detail

Cornicing, dado (chair) rails and baseboards were originally devised as framing devices for areas of the wall covered in paper or fabric. In Victorian decorating schemes, for example, there may have been a decorative paper frieze between cornice and picture rail, another type of wallpaper pattern between picture rail and dado, and a heavier, more robust patterned paper below the dado.

In addition to their decorative role, details also had a practical function. Cornicing conceals the superficial cracking that appears when the wall surface meets the ceiling. Dado rails were designed specifically to prevent damage to papered surfaces in the days when chairs were commonly pushed back against the wall when not in use. Baseboards perform a similar task by protecting that margin of the wall most prone to scrapes and other damage.

Because details such as cornices, picture rails and baseboards interrupt the wall, breaking what would otherwise be a smooth surface into defined sections, they can work against a feeling of spaciousness and make a room feel more enclosed.

1 Simply removing doors and architraves can make a space seem less cluttered. The distinction between different areas remains, but the effect is more spacious and open. Here, a sliding panel separates a kitchen from the dining area, allowing kitchen activity to be hidden during meals.

2 Shadow gapping entails stopping the drywalling on a wall just before the floor – a neat contemporary detail (or absence of one).

2

■ **Avoid calling attention to it** This can be achieved very simply by painting cornicing, baseboards, doors and other woodwork the same color as walls and ceilings. Painting the entire wall the same color makes detailing recede into the background to a greater degree.

■ **Remove unnecessary features** Now that we don't routinely push chairs back to the wall or cover walls with damask, the dado is largely redundant in practical terms. A ceiling rosette can look rather forlorn in the absence of a central light. As central lighting is one of the least successful ways of lighting small spaces, you may wish to remove the rosette as well.

■ **Remove details altogether** If you are undertaking extensive renovation and remodeling work that involves creating new partition walls or openings, and hence necessitates considerable drywalling and redecorating, think about removing existing details at the same time.

Shadow gapping

One particular technique that both minimizes architectural detail and provides a neat finishing touch is shadow gapping. This involves stopping the drywall a little short of the floor or ceiling so that there is a slight gap between the two surfaces. The resulting shadow gives crispness of definition and creates the illusion that the wall is hovering over the floor. In practical terms, it also means that in the absence of baseboards the lower edge of the drywall is not exposed to damage. Generally, the gap should be wide enough to take the crevice tool of a vacuum cleaner.

Shadow gapping is carried out using a profiled strip of metal or metal mesh that supports the lower edge of the drywall. Not many drywallers are familiar with shadow gapping and the technique must be executed well to be successful, so it is best to ask around if you intend to have such work done.

1 A contemporary steel fireplace with integral flue makes a dramatic statement suspended in the middle of a living area, over a circular hearth made of heatproof material.
2 A concrete fireplace surround provides a modern update on a traditional period feature. The mantelpiece extends past the chimney breast to form a shelf below the window.
3 A neat wood-burning modern stove set into the wall, with a recess beneath for firewood. Always have such features professionally installed and regularly inspected: they require proper ventilation.

1

2

Fireplaces and stoves

There are few people who do not welcome the comfort of a real fire and appreciate the convivial atmosphere it creates. While central heating has reduced our dependence on fire for warmth, its psychological appeal is undiminished. A fireplace is a natural focal point, a hospitable gathering point and a welcome replacement for a TV.

In small homes, particularly those converted from older houses, fireplaces – and fireplace surrounds in particular – may occupy valuable wall space that could be put to better use. While you may wish to retain a fireplace in a living area where people naturally gather, additional fireplaces in bedrooms, for example, are likely to be left unused.

Removing a fireplace

If there is an existing fireplace surround, call in a salvage expert or fireplace specialist to remove it for you. Period fireplaces – even basic tiled surrounds dating from the 1930s and 1940s – are much sought after and you can be well compensated. Don't simply hack away at the fireplace, or you may damage the tiles, stone or marble.

Bear in mind that the chimney breast of a house is a structural element. You cannot remove one without causing a great deal of disruption and without putting some form of compensatory support in its place. Consult an architect or structural engineer.

The simplest way of treating a redundant fireplace is to block it up and decorate it so that it appears to

If there is an existing surround, call in a salvage expert or fireplace specialist to remove it for you – period fireplaces are much sought after and you could be well compensated

3

form part of the wall. Chimneys and rooms require ventilation, so it is essential that you ensure that air flow won't be compromised.

Alternatively, you can make use of the recess as a storage area and fill it with shelves, an approach that is particularly useful in children's rooms.

Contemporary fireplaces

An ornate fireplace surround can be overly dominant if you are adopting a reticent approach to detailing elsewhere in the interior. In this case it can be very effective to treat the hearth as a simple "firebox," rendered a dark color inside and neatly framed by the wall. Raised fireplaces are also very effective, but bear in mind that heat rises, so you would be advised

not to raise a hearth too far from the floor, or you will be warming the ceiling rather than yourself.

Specialists in modern fireplaces produce a number of designs that deliver all the home comforts of a traditional fire but are much more discreet. Another alternative is to opt for a gas or electric fireplace where the flames are visible through a glass door.

Fire safety and preparation
- When you are renovating an old fireplace, check that the chimney or flue is lined and that the lining is intact. A chimney sweep can carry out a smoke test to determine if there are any deficiencies in the lining that could allow poisonous gases, such as carbon monoxide, to seep into living or sleeping areas.
- Always have chimneys cleaned regularly, ideally at the start of every winter season.
- Use a fireguard if there are children in the home and never leave children unattended in a room where a fire is burning.
- Install smoke alarms.

Scale & Proportion

1 Ever since technological developments have produced glass that is strong enough to walk on, architects and designers have experimented with the exciting potential of glass floors. Here, a section of floor has been replaced with a glass panel that allows light into the lower level.

2 A large expanse of glass forms a bedroom wall, enhancing the sense of space. The room appears much larger than it actually is because of the borrowed view.

3 Double-width openings connect a kitchen with a dining area and the dining area with the hall and stairs. If you are creating new openings, you may need to install a support beam to compensate for the area of lost wall.

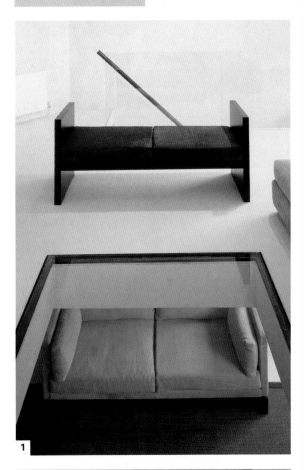

Openings

Small spaces naturally feel less confined when there are views – both interior and exterior – that allow the eye to travel onward. In most cases these vistas will be provided by conventional openings such as doors and windows. Opening up on a larger scale by removing all, or a portion, of a dividing wall can also enhance the sense of space.

Openings play a critical role in admitting natural light and air to the interior. The quality of light is indivisible from the quality of space; the better lit, the more uplifting an area will be. Similarly, free circulation of air not only promotes healthy living conditions, it also adds a feeling of vitality and freshness to the interior.

Changes to windows

Most living areas – or "habitable rooms," in planning terms – are lit by at least one window. Although kitchens, bathrooms and cloakrooms can be fully internal, they do require some form of ventilation in the absence of a window that can be opened.

Changing windows or installing new openings varies in complexity and scope of work. Because exterior walls are an important supporting element, alterations to openings in those walls can have structural implications. Such improvements, however, can make a vast difference to the way you experience your home, in both practical and aesthetic terms.

■ **Lengthening existing exterior windows** This is the simplest type of alteration that you can make to exterior windows because no structural work is required. It is fairly straightforward, for example, to remove the portion of wall beneath the lower sill of an existing window to create a larger opening.

■ **Widening existing exterior windows** Enlarging windows widthwise or making a single large window from a pair of smaller ones, for example, does have structural implications. In this case a rolled-steel joist (RSJ) or some other support will need to be installed over the new opening to compensate for the loss of load-bearing wall. By widening (and lengthening) existing windows, you can create a new means of access to a patio, deck, balcony or garden via French doors or sliding doors.

■ **Installing new openings** If your home is poorly lit, this alteration can be a good option. Issues of orientation and privacy come into play – it is best to site the window on the side of your home that receives good natural light (west- or south-facing in the northern hemisphere; east- or north-facing in the southern hemisphere). Similarly, think about what the new window will reveal. If the view is poor or if you are likely to be overlooked by neighbors, you may wish to consider filling the opening with semi-translucent or stained glass. All new exterior openings involve structural work and a beam will need to be installed over the window.

■ **Creating new interior openings** Interior windows provide tantalizing glimpses from area to area without committing you to a fully open-concept arrangement. They are a particularly good way of connecting windowless kitchens or bathrooms to areas that are better lit, effectively "borrowing" light and spreading it around. Creating an internal window in a partition wall is straight-forward; if you are making an opening in a structural wall, however, you will need to install a beam or compensatory structural element. It is not always easy to tell which walls are simple partition walls and which are doing the more important work of supporting the structure of your house, so it is essential to consult an architect or engineer. New interior openings can be any shape – round, horizontal, vertical, square – and either left fully open or filled with glass (clear, translucent or colored).

■ **Installing top lighting** Roof windows and other forms of top lighting have a dramatic effect on spatial quality (see page 43).

Changes to doors

Conventional doors often do not make the most of available space, either in terms of scale or in means of operation. Quite simple alterations can give you more room to maneuver, while changes that involve increasing the size of the opening offer similar benefits as alterations to window size and shape.

Options

■ **Widening existing exterior doors** As is the case with windows, widening an existing door in an exterior wall entails structural change. Turning a standard door into French doors can improve access to garden areas or decks; you will need to install a joist or beam over the top of the widened opening. Alternatively, you can replace an entire end wall with sliding glass doors. Such an arrangement, as well as improving the quality and levels of light and promoting the circulation of air, will have the effect of dissolving the boundary between indoors and out.

■ **Replacing solid doors with glass doors** This tends to be an option that is more practical for interior doors; an exterior front door demands a greater degree of security than most types of glass doors can supply. Interior glass doors allow light to spill through from area to area within the home.

■ **Extending interior doors from floor to ceiling** A door of standard size and proportion defines an area as a separate room; replace it with a sliding panel that extends to ceiling height, and the effect is to allow ceiling and floor planes to run through a space unobstructed.

■ **Sliding doors or panels** are more space-saving than doors that open inward.

Screens and partitions

Like sliding doors, screens can be used to partition space in a flexible way. Screens enable you to expose certain areas of activity – such as a built-in

home office, for example – when you need access to them and conceal them from view the rest of the time.

Consider different types of material. If you prefer a self-effacing look, choose a material that blends in with the wall or can be decorated to match. For a lighter, less imposing look, opt for translucent materials such as glass, plexiglass and glass block or brick.

Types of screens and partitions

The simplest screen is the freestanding version, which can either be bought from furniture shops or second-hand outlets, or custom-made by a carpenter. Many contemporary designs have a pleasing sculptural quality that adds a certain dynamic to the space. A

For a lighter, less imposing look, opt for translucent materials such as glass, plexiglass or glass block or brick

1 Flush panel doors are less intrusive than conventional paneled designs. These doors appear as part of the wall when closed. Other panels conceal built-in storage.
2 A sleeping area in an open-concept space is screened by large panels of translucent glass to allow light through while maintaining a necessary level of privacy.
3 A floor-to-ceiling sliding panel separates a bathroom and home office from the bedroom. Such panels, when shut, are more self-effacing than conventional doors.

similar effect can be achieved using portable room dividers that double up as a place for storage and display. The advantage of these options is that they do not commit you to a fixed furniture layout.

More permanent arrangements include sliding panels, screens that fold or accordion back into a slot in the wall and panels that can be lifted up like a garage door. Such fixtures are useful when it comes to concealing built-in functional spaces, such as a kitchen area, within a multipurpose space.

Solid partitions range from walls judiciously placed to subdivide a space into separate rooms to half-height and half-width partitions. In tightly planned areas, such as bathrooms, moving a partition wall even by a matter of an inch or two can often make all the difference between a layout that is workable and one that is too cramped to be practical. Creating a new solid partition wall involves building work but has no structural implications. Remember that solid partition walls do not need to be straight; a curve, while costlier to construct, introduces a great sense of vitality to the space.

1 A good solution for open-concept layouts is to centralize plumbing and utility service areas. Here, a bathroom and shower are grouped within the core, with integral clothes storage built in to one side.

Open-concept layouts

One of the most common design strategies for small spaces is to adopt an open-concept layout, removing as many partitions or dividing walls as is practical to create a single multipurpose area. Instead of a series of small rooms connected by hallways, and each with an access door, there is a free flow of space, accommodating many of the functions and activities of everyday life.

Open-concept layouts have much to offer. It is important to be aware, however, that there are downsides to the arrangement, and that simply removing as many interior walls as possible will not necessarily give you a better quality of space.

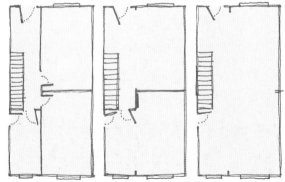

■ Taking down walls through is one way to give older properties a more contemporary feel. You can absorb hallways within the main rooms or remove all the interior partition walls to provide one open space. Bear in mind that while you gain extra floor area you will lose wall space, which may affect furniture and heating register placement and storage possibilities. Open-concept spaces need careful consideration to avoid becoming featureless.

1

Pros

■ Opening up the layout will not result in additional room per se, but your home will feel more spacious. Views and vistas will be enhanced.

■ In a townhouse property, with windows overlooking the street and yard, removing the dividing walls between the front and rear rooms will result in a better quality of light.

■ Open-concept layouts force you to think more carefully about how best to accommodate different activities in the same space, perhaps by grouping plumbing and utility service areas into a more space-efficient central core.

■ Absorbing hallways and other circulation areas into the main living space can simplify routes.

■ Open layouts are more in tune with the fluidity of contemporary lifestyles – there is no need for a formal dining room if you like to entertain your friends to an impromptu supper in the kitchen.

■ You add the thickness of the removed walls to your space.

Cons

■ Open-concept layouts can be noisy unless you decorate and furnish them with materials such as carpet and fabrics that have sound-absorbing qualities.

■ Without proper planning , there is a risk that different activities might impinge upon each other in an open-concept space.

■ Fully open layouts do not provide any truly private or contemplative space. If you are sharing your home with a partner, each of you will want some space to call your own.

■ Removing partitions and dividing walls can look awkward if the resulting space has two chimney breasts lined up along one wall. It is often more comfortable visually, in these cases, to retain a portion of the dividing wall – a suggestion of former enclosure – rather than remove it completely.

■ In a fully open-concept area, the loss of wall space can limit your opportunities for creating built-in storage.

Structural considerations

Before you go ahead and knock down a wall – or ask the builders to do it for you – you need to be clear which walls are structural and which are merely partitions. A structural wall will be performing an important supporting role, carrying some of the load of the floor above. If you make an opening in a structural wall or knock it down completely, you have to put a beam, joist or supporting column in its place. Partition walls, on the other hand – which are often made of studwork – simply divide space and do not hold anything up. They tend to sound hollow when tapped. Always consult an architect or building professional before carrying out these types of alterations.

Scale & Proportion

1 A glass roof provides direct natural light from above – a real feel-good factor. Such roofs are best if they are slightly sloped, so that water and leaves cannot settle on top and spoil the view.
2 A sleeping platform inserted in a high-ceilinged space is screened with a huge panel hoisted by rope and pulley.

3 An open-tread staircase allows light to spill down from openings on the level above. White decor helps to spread the light around.

Volume

Architects and other spatial designers often talk – and think – about space in terms of "volume." While this particular spatial concept does not form part of most people's everyday vocabulary, all of us can appreciate what it means. Take the example of two rooms of identical length and width, but which differ in ceiling height. The room with the higher ceiling will inevitably feel more spacious and more uplifting, even though the floor area is no greater.

Even when your home is on the small side, variations in volume can help introduce a richness of spatial experience, where relatively low and intimate spaces give way to soaring high ceilings. In some cases it can be worth sacrificing a degree of floor area on an upper story to generate that sense of expansion.

Changes to volume

■ Raising a portion of the floor up a few steps in an open-concept area can serve to underscore a shift in activity. For example, you might create a raised kitchen within a multipurpose space that includes a living/relaxing area.

■ If you are converting an attic or loft, or a similar space with high ceilings, it can be worth grouping several functions into a "service core" that stops short of the ceiling, in order to preserve the sense of volume. For example, you might construct a kitchen/bathroom/storage area that provides a sleeping space on the upper level.

■ Sometimes, lowering a ceiling is necessary to correct proportions. If you have sectioned off one portion of a high-ceilinged bedroom to make a bathroom, for instance, the resulting space might feel awkward. Dropping the ceiling adjusts the proportion to a more human scale.

■ Losing a small portion of floor area on an upper story to make a high-ceilinged area creates drama.

In certain circumstances, lowering a ceiling is necessary to correct proportions and adjust them to a more human scale

Top lighting

Light that comes from above is naturally space-enhancing and uplifting, and exposes an interior space to all the evocative variations in light level that one would experience outdoors. Top lighting is of particular benefit in homes with few windows and where creating new ones in external walls is problematic. Think carefully about siting to maximize the effect.

Good sites for top lighting include

- Over a staircase, to spill the light down through several levels
- Over a landing
- Over a bathtub
- Over a bed

Types of top lighting

- **Openable windows set into the roof** These are standard for loft or attic conversions. Many tilt or pivot to make cleaning easier.
- **Skylights** Various versions of roof windows, often installed in flat sections of roof.
- **Clerestory windows** Fixed or openable windows, generally horizontal, set high up the wall in high-ceilinged spaces.
- **Light tubes** An ingenious system for bringing natural light into dark internal areas, the light tube consists of a surface-mounted skylight connected to a reflective tube that bounces light down its interior to emerge at a ceiling-mounted interior skylight.
- **Glass roofs** These are particular useful for sunrooms or sideways additions.
- **Glass floor sections and upper walkways** Using glass on lofts and upper levels allows light to spill down from level to level.
- **Sidewalk lights** Glass bricks or strips set into a sidewalk allow natural light into basement rooms below.

Glass

It is vital to choose the right type of glass for the application in question.

- For flooring, stairs and walkways, use panels of toughened glass, comprising a ¾ in. (2 cm) top layer laminated to a ½ in. (1 cm) base, with sandblasted friction bars.
- To prevent heat loss from glass roofs, use highly insulating low-E (or low-emissivity) glass, which is coated with thin layers of silver oxide to reflect heat back into the interior.
- For doors and screens, use toughened shatterproof glass that fractures into harmless pebbles.
- Special glazing materials are now available, including glass with built-in security sensors and glass that changes from opaque to clear at the flick of a switch.

Stairs, Halls & Landings

Stairs, halls and landings are connecting areas – what architects term "circulation space." If you live in an older property, the chances are that those connecting areas may be on the generous side – in some Victorian houses, they may account for almost a third of the total volume. Adjusting or redesigning connecting areas can go a long way toward making better overall use of the space at your disposal. The first step is to take a look at the way you move around your home, and within individual rooms or areas. We generally like to take the easy way out – or the shortest distance from A to B. In some cases, however, our homes are not planned and laid out to facilitate this, so simple chores such as bringing in the groceries or taking out the garbage entail countless trips up and down stairs and along hallways. When you have limited living and working space at your disposal, routes should be as simple and direct as possible.

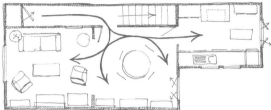

Make a sketch plan

Draw up a basic sketch plan of each level of your home (see page 23). Take measurements of each room or area and draw the plan to scale, so that you get some idea of proportion and spatial layout. Mark exterior and interior doors and other openings on the plan.

Analyze your routes

Use the plan or plans to work out how you commonly move from room to room or area to area. Just like the bare patches in the park that reveal where people stray from the path to take a shortcut, areas of wear on the floor can demonstrate where indoor traffic is greatest. Mark the routes on the plan and try to work out if there are ways in which these might be simplified, or if there are other changes that you could make to improve the use of space.

Consider the following

■ If a room or area has a choice of access doors, you may find that you tend to enter by one door rather than the other. If so, the second door is redundant and could be blocked up to provide more useful wall area on both sides.

■ Is it easy to move from place to place or are there obstacles in your way? Cramped or awkward connecting spaces reinforce the feeling that your home is too small to be comfortable. Many circulation areas are used as dumping grounds for possessions that are en route to their permanent homes. Instigating a clean sweep can make an enormous difference to the way your home functions and feels.

■ Consider whether changing the way a door is hung will improve matters. For example, if you have a very small bathroom, a door that opens inward will compromise the sense of space even further. Rehanging a door so it opens the other way or replacing it with a sliding door or pocket can make a surprising amount of difference.

■ Imagine yourself performing a variety of routine household tasks, such as getting the mail, answering the telephone or taking out the garbage. Could interior or exterior doors be better sited so you can carry out these activities more efficiently and seamlessly?

1

1 A spiral staircase has undeniable appeal and a certain theatricality, as well as being space-saving. There are a variety of designs in different materials, but metal is a popular option. If you are intending to install a period cast-iron staircase, check that the floor structure can bear the additional load.

Space-saving stairs

Conventional staircases take up a great deal of room – not only floor space, but areas devoted to landings. If you are converting an older property, you may wish to replace a standard staircase with a space-saving one. If you are converting an attic or loft, or installing a loft level in a high-ceilinged space, space-saving stairs can also represent an efficient option.

Sources include specialized staircase manu-facturers (many of whom supply stairs in ready-to-assemble form to your own specification), custom staircase builders and architectural salvage yards. Alternatively, if you are hiring an architect to redesign your home, he or she will be able to come up with a solution that suits your particular requirements.

Types of design

■ **Spiral stairs** The spiral staircase, turning either in a continuous curve or in a series of angled steps around a central support, is both a dramatic feature and a practical space-saving option. Ornate period examples are available from architectural salvage yards and from specialized manufacturers; these tend to be made of cast iron and are very heavy, which means you will need to check whether the floor structure can bear the weight. Much simpler contemporary designs are produced in a range of materials, with the supports and balusters generally made of wood or metal and treads available in wood, metal, marble and even glass. Some spiral stairs come complete with "universal" platforms to suit either circular or square stairwells and allow you to adjust the rotation – clockwise or counterclockwise – on site to suit the specific location. Even more space-saving are half-spiral designs.

■ **Modular stairs** A variety of designs allow multiple configurations, either straight flights, or L or U shapes. Some ready-to-assemble stairs can be adjusted on site to take account of anomalies of measurement, which would otherwise spell disaster in the case of a

2 An open ladder-like staircase with a central support is pitched at a steeper angle than conventional stairs, which saves space in the level below.
3 Paddle steps, or "monk's stairs," as they are sometimes known, are another space-saving option, though only for the sure-footed.

4 Do not neglect the storage potential offered by stairs. Stair treads can be transformed into drawers or cubbyholes for storing a range of different items. Here, a stair drawer is used, appropriately enough, for shoe storage.

If you are converting an attic or loft, or installing a loft level in a high-ceilinged space, space-saving stairs can also represent an efficient option

Meeting regulations

A number of regulations are in place concerning the design and construction of stairs for domestic use, including the height of the rise and the angle of the staircase. Some commercially available staircases meet building regulations (or "code"); some do not. You will need to check with your local planning department to determine whether the design you are planning to install meets with their approval.

Safety

Friction bars on metal or glass treads prevent slipping; non-slip finishes are also available. Stairs with extreme angles or tight spirals may pose a danger to the very young, the elderly or the infirm. Secured ladders providing access to platform or bunk beds must be strong and firmly anchored.

custom-made stair. Very narrow designs are available with paddle treads.

■ **Open or cantilevered stairs** Stairs with open flights and those cantilevered from the wall are more space-enhancing than space-saving, but still provide minimal interruption in an open-concept space.

■ **Loft ladders** Commercially available loft ladders come in a variety of designs – folding, heavy duty, retractable and sliding – in wood or metal. These are best used for occasional access to a storage area rather than on an everyday basis.

■ **Custom-made designs** Many architects have produced ingenious solutions to staircase design, including alternate paddle steps with integral storage cubicles.

Making use of circulation space

The prime function of circulation space is to provide access to different areas in the home. But that does not mean that halls, stairs and landings cannot serve other functions as well, both practical and aesthetic.

Landings

In older properties, landings can be fairly generous in size. Provided you can still move safely from level to level, there are a number of ways in which you can make practical use of what might otherwise be wasted space.

Potential uses

■ In many homes, bathrooms are situated on the landing level. If your bathroom is small and adjacent to a landing, you might find that you could move the bathroom wall forward into the landing space without impinging on key traffic routes and vastly improve the workability of the layout of fixtures in the bathroom.

■ Landings can also provide convenient locations for storage. You might build cupboards on each side to accommodate your clothes and shoes, or use a freestanding chest or armoire to hold linens, bedding and towels. Alternatively, many landings make excellent places to keep books, either on built-in shelving or in freestanding bookcases.

■ Very spacious landings can also be pressed into service as working areas. If your main living area is multipurpose, a quiet corner of a landing can provide the necessary psychological separation for work. Installing a skylight over the landing will improve the quality of natural light dramatically and create a sense of expansiveness that aids concentration.

1

2

1 Deep, boxed built-in storage frames an entrance, providing a place to keep outdoor wear, along with room for display – a good place to check appointments on a calendar.
2 A neat home office has been slotted into a landing. Built-in cupboards create a recess for the desktop.
3 Generous landings can make surprisingly good locations for home offices, particularly if the quality of natural light is good, as here.

■ Think about using hallways and stairs as places for display. If individual rooms are small, they can rapidly be overwhelmed by collections of photographs and paintings. You can, on the other hand, treat a hallway as a gallery without running the risk of making the walls close in. Further, displays in circulation areas enliven what might otherwise be neutral space, and the fact that one appreciates such displays only in transition keeps them fresh for longer.

■ Similarly, if you are adopting a restrained, neutral approach to decorating elsewhere in the home, the hallway can be a good place to introduce a strong color that will give you a little jolt of pleasure as you move from place to place. As is the case with displays, you will experience the color only momentarily, which means you are less likely to tire of it.

■ Larger halls, landings and understair spaces can be made more practical as places for storage or as compact working areas.

3

Stairs, Halls & Landings

1 Make use of understair areas for built-in storage. These stepped cupboards usefully house a variety of possessions. Cupboards such as these can be surprisingly capacious.
2 Another variation on the theme shows individual understair lockers used to store cups and dishes in a kitchen.
3 A suspended staircase allows enough space for access to the fridge built into the end wall.

4 One of the most successful ways of taming clutter is to organize possessions in a series of discreet cabinets. These floor-to-ceiling cabinets lining one wall of a hallway relieve pressure on space in adjoining rooms. A neat row of pegs on the opposite wall provides a place for hanging up bags and coats. If your hallway is wide enough, it is worth considering devoting part of it to built in storage.

Understairs

The area below the stairs is a useful between-space that is often ignored in many homes – or, if it is not ignored, it tends to serve as a dumping ground for belongings that you do not know what to do with or cannot find a home for. Instead of consigning all your clutter to this one spot, it is well worth taking the trouble to design it properly, as either a storage or a working area.

There are many different ways in which you can make efficient use of understair space:

■ One of the simplest is to shelve the recess and install doors on the front. The resulting cupboard space can be used to house a wide variety of possessions, from cleaning tools and products to boots, shoes, sports gear and bulky supplies.

■ A series of stepped cupboards or pull-out racks can also be a practical way of exploiting every square inch of the space.

■ Understair spaces are good locations for wine racks, as they are out of the way of main traffic routes, but still accessible.

■ A generous-sized area under the stairs can be outfitted with a built in desk and shelving to create a work area.

■ Do not forget the stairs themselves. There are many ingenious storage possibilities – for example, pull-out drawers built in under stair treads.

If you need to store bulky items such as bicycles in the hall, invest in a strong racking system

4

Halls

Entrance halls provide an important mediating zone between indoors and out; between the privacy of your home and the public world outside. All too often, however, especially if space is tight elsewhere in the home, they come to resemble the front line of chaos. If you trip over a bicycle every time you leave your home, or return to the depressing sight of a jumble of unanswered letters and junk mail, it is time to rethink how to best use the space.

Seamless storage cupboards can be built into wide hallways to store clutter from adjacent living areas. If possible, devote an entire wall to such a solution. You can customize the interior of the cabinets according to what you are storing – with rails or pegs for hanging up outdoor wear, shelves for holding files, and cubbyholes for boots and shoes.

Another solution is to line a wall with open shelving to take all of your books, CDs and other media accessories.

If you need to store bulky items such as bicycles in the hall, invest in a strong racking system, either to hang the bikes on the wall or to store them overhead.

DECO

PART 1
MAKING THE MOST OF SMALL SPACES

RATING & FURNISHING

Color, Texture & Pattern

Small spaces need careful thought and planning to work efficiently and to serve your needs with the minimum of compromise. Once you have sorted out the practicalities to the best of your abilities and to the full potential of the space, it is time to put your personal stamp on it and make it a place you love.

How you decorate your home is all about creative expression. In a small space, however, judicious decorating choices can also help generate a feeling of airiness and expansion that makes the most of what you have.

Of course, there is another approach, and that is to defy the spatial limitations and choose colors – and even patterns – that would normally be used in more generous surroundings. I would not necessarily advise adopting this approach throughout your home, but in measured doses it can deliver a great sense of fun and vitality.

1 Color achieves added impact when it is used in small doses. This room, chiefly decorated in white and neutral shades, comes to life with the injection of bright red, as displayed in the chair upholstery and the bowl. Using color as accent means you can change displays easily and alter the mood.

■ Because decorating is a relatively quick and straightforward business compared with other forms of home improvement, many people make the mistake of rushing decisions without properly considering their impact. The result is all too often a paint scheme that just doesn't look quite right or a flooring material that is much darker in situ than you had expected from the sample at the store. Like design, successful decorating requires a period of assessment, weighing of options and quite a lot of on-site viewing of samples.

■ Think about your home as a whole, not merely as a number of linked areas or separate rooms. In a small space, abrupt changes of decor can undermine any sense of unity. This is not to say that every room or area should display the same decorating choices, but there must be a consistent theme that holds it all together. This is all the more important where space is divided flexibly to permit views and vistas from area to area.

■ The floor represents one of the greatest surface areas in the home and is a powerful unifier. In a small space it is often best to base your decorating scheme around the choice of flooring material. Extending the same flooring right through your home or restricting yourself to flooring materials that are very similar tonally is a tried-and-true space-enhancing strategy.

■ Before you commit yourself to a specific material, take home some samples and live with them for a while to judge their impact. What looked right in the store under bright artificial light may appear very different at home, under varying conditions of natural light. For the same reason, try out paint colors using sample containers of your chosen shade. Paint substantial patches on several walls to gauge the effect.

■ A good way of visualizing a scheme is to assemble swatches and samples on a mood board. This helps you think in concrete terms right from the start.

Color, Texture & Pattern

1 In a small space, color is often best used as a feature or accent. Strips of vivid color enliven a recess in one wall; the effect is repeated in the mirror at the end of the otherwise all-white kitchen.
2 Blue is a distancing shade that can help make a room seem more spacious. It is, however, chilly, which means you need to use it in situations where the quality of light is warm, not cool – in the northern hemisphere, that means south- and west-facing aspects.
3 Color is particularly effective when it is used in combination with light. Transparent colored glass or colored plexiglass panels, like the ones here, have enhanced luminosity.

Using color

Color has a powerful effect on our mood and on the atmosphere created within a given space. The colors at the so-called "warm" end of the spectrum – yellows, reds and oranges – are "advancing" colors, which means they tend to leap out at you: hence the red "Stop" sign or the red "Sale" sign. There is a good reason for this. Red, which corresponds to the longer wavelengths of light, requires the maximum adjustment from our eyes, which is why we experience this particular color as arousing or exciting – literally eye-catching. Green, a color that falls in the middle of the spectrum, is restful because our eyes do not have to adjust very much to see it. The cooler colors – blue, blue-grays and violets – are short wavelength colors and are therefore distancing and soothing in effect.

Added to these physical responses are more subjective, cultural or emotional associations. Some people are instinctively drawn to warm, spicy colors; others to cooler, more calming shades; some to both.

■ **Tonal difference** Colors that reflect natural light to a greater degree – which include white and colors that contain a high proportion of white – tend to make spaces seem larger. Dark colors that absorb light make the walls close in.

■ **Warm versus cool** In decorating terms, warm colors, such as yellow, red and orange tones, generate a sense of intimacy and enclosure. Cool colors, on the other hand, such as shades of blues, blue-gray and violet,

Never commit yourself to a paint shade without testing a sample first – certain colors appear darker and more intense painted on an expanse of wall than they do on chips and swatches

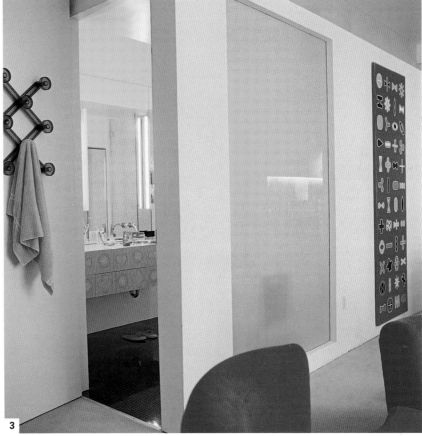

3

are distancing, which gives them an obvious relevance for small space decorating schemes.

■ **Complementary** Colors that sit directly opposite each other on the color wheel are said to be complementary. Blue and orange, yellow and purple, and red and green are the standard complementary pairs. Basing a decoration scheme around a pair of these colors, using different tones from light to dark, is a fail-safe approach.

■ **Edgy** Turquoise, blue-gray and lavender are all shades that sit on the border between one color and the next. Technically, such shades are known as "tertiary colors." Their effect in decorating is to bring an edgy, luminous quality to an interior, which can be very effective in small spaces.

■ **Orientation** You should make all color decisions based on the quality of natural light that a room receives. Areas that receive warm natural light (south- or west-facing aspects in the northern hemisphere; the reverse in the southern) can take cooler shades than areas that face north or east. Add a chilly color to a room that is already dark or northlit and the effect will be clinical and dreary.

■ **Testing** Never commit yourself to a paint shade without testing a sample first. Certain colors appear darker and more intense painted on an expanse of wall than they do on small paint chips and swatches. Try out the color on walls that receive natural light and those that do not and assess how it looks at different times of the day.

1

1 All-white decoration is a tried-and-true means of enhancing space and making the most of natural light. Here, the natural tones of the polished wood floor add depth of character to the white decorating scheme.
2 A blue-painted panel injects color interest in an otherwise neutral scheme. There is a range of evocative shades of blues to choose from, including blue-gray, blue-green and lavender, all of which are edgy and luminous.

Space-enhancing color

When your home is on the small side, it is generally best to opt for background colors that both reflect light and are inherently distancing in effect. This serves to push back the walls and create a sense of freshness and airiness.

White

Most people's first choice when it comes to small space decorating is white. White walls, pale floors and white soft furnishings make the most of available natural light and generate a serene and contemplative mood. White, however, is not necessarily an easy option. Slight differences in aspect, finish and tone can make the difference between an all-white scheme that is successful and one that is banal and insipid.

Tone

Small variations in tone can make a great deal of difference when you are basing a decorating scheme around an extensive use of white. Pure white is an absolute that is hard to achieve. Many commercial paints, especially those advertised as "brilliant white," include a small proportion of blue for the "whiter than white" effect. In rooms that receive bright natural light, such whites look crisp and fresh and can be very invigorating. In darker surroundings, however, they will look chilly and gloomy. A creamier white is a much better solution for areas where the quality of natural light is less than ideal, such as in basements.

Finish and texture

Different finishes will also affect the appearance of white. Matte, chalky white works well with natural materials and rugged textures. Mid-sheen finishes are more light-enhancing and make a good accompaniment to soft, sensuous materials such as upholstery fabrics and carpeting. Highly glossy or lacquered finishes are the most reflective and give additional crispness and definition in combination with glass, mirror or polished metal.

Matching

If you are opting for an all-white scheme, as opposed to simply using white as the principal background color for walls and ceilings, you need to be aware that the closer you can match the various shades of white used in the interior, the better the final result will be. Off-white next to pure white simply looks dirty.

Maintenance

There is no getting around the fact that white interiors demand extra maintenance to stay looking good. If you have children or pets, white upholstery is probably not advisable, unless the covers are loose and washable – have more than one set if possible. Expect to decorate more often.

2

Blues

Blues and other shades at the cool end of the spectrum have a natural role in small space decorating. Blue is a distancing color – think of the blue on the horizon – which means that walls or other surfaces painted or colored blue tend to look farther away than they really are. Use blue in areas that receive good natural light. In dark rooms blue can be depressing. Blue and white is a fresh and cheerful combination; white walls can be partnered with light or mid-blue kitchen cabinets, for example. Light blues are more space-enhancing than darker shades. Avoid pastels, however, which tend to look wishy-washy. Blue-grays, blue-greens and pale violet or lavender – shades that sit on the edge between warm and cool colors – are luminous and full of vitality.

Color, Texture & Pattern

1

1 White or neutral schemes run the risk of looking a little ethereal or insipid without textural contrast. Great care has been taken in this interior to match whites and to contrast textures, with rough finishes offset by smooth and glossy ones, and matte materials with those that are semi-transparent.
2 Natural surfaces and finishes have inherent compatibility. The actual tonal range in this bathroom is fairly limited, but the contrast of concrete, wood, stainless steel and mirror gives added vitality.

Textural contrast

A key element in successful small space decorating, textural contrast implies the use of different materials, going beyond superficial cover-ups with paint or paper. Texture is the physical, tangible aspect of decorating, dictating not only the way a surface appears, but also how it feels, sounds and wears. Visually, textural characteristics may range from subtle shifts in the ability of different materials to reflect light to more overt patterning in the form of wood grain, for example, or how tiles are laid.

In small spaces, where strong color and busy patterns can be too overwhelming, textural variety adds a sense of depth and character that prevents the overall effect from being bland. From the start, when you are considering your scheme as a whole, try to think in terms of surfaces and finishes as well as colors. Building up a sympathetic palette of materials will ensure the resulting scheme has vitality.

Natural materials, many of which are fairly neutral in tone, are often preferable to artificial ones, even the upmarket, successful lookalikes. This is because natural materials age well, bearing the marks of wear without appearing irredeemably degraded. A worn vinyl floor, for example, is an eyesore; an old oak floor, lovingly tended over the years, has charm and integrity.

Ringing the changes with materials has practical implications. If every surface is hard and reflective, your home will be noisy and wearing; uniformly soft materials will be soporific. Some balance is required.

2

Flooring

Textural contrast is particularly effective underfoot. If you restrict your choice of flooring to a narrow range of light or neutral tones, you can still vary the material according to the practical requirements of a particular location. For example, pale wood flooring in a living area might be combined with a natural-fiber covering on the stairs and pale ceramic tiles in the kitchen and bathroom.

Reflective surfaces

Stainless steel, glass, mirror and highly polished materials, such as lacquered wood, polished granite and glazed tiles, are space-enhancing because they make the most of natural light. Many of these do, however, require greater maintenance than non-reflective materials to keep them free from smudges.

Comfort zone

Pay particular attention to materials and surfaces that you touch on a regular basis. Upholstery, cushion and pillow covers, and bed and bath linens in natural fibers deliver greater sensuous pleasure than artificial fabrics. Thick soft towels, fine cotton sheets, wool throws and crisp linen covers lend a sense of generosity to your home – all the more welcome if space is limited.

Color, Texture & Pattern

1 One way of using strong color in a small space is to limit it to a self-contained room. This nursery in a converted attic space is painted an uplifting shade of sunshine yellow – a happy, cheerful color for a child to wake up to.

Bold statements

Living in small spaces does not preclude you from making bold decorating statements. Strong colors and patterns are inherently uplifting and it would be a pity to forgo the visual delight they can bring to a scheme simply because space is restricted. Nevertheless, such vibrant elements require careful handling at the best of times; in small spaces extra care is needed.

I would suggest that if you are going to use strong color or overt patterning you think about allowing plenty of breathing space so the effect is not too overwhelming. There are several ways in which this can be achieved.

■ **Accent** Both color and pattern can be used as accents – for example, in details or accessories. Cushions and pillows, throws, bed linens, upholstery and similar soft furnishings provide the opportunity to display strong colors or patterns in a limited way, without compromising the sense of space. Bright red cushions or a single patterned upholstered chair add a jolt of interest and vitality when backgrounds are plain and neutral – as do decorative objects and pictures. A particular benefit of this approach is that such elements are easy to change if and when you get tired of a certain color or print. Many kitchen appliances, such as fridges and stoves, now come in a choice of strong colors, and while you would not replace such items on a regular basis, they can also be used to introduce liveliness to an otherwise reticent decorating scheme.

■ **Focal point** The second strategy is to use color or pattern as a focal point. One wall or partition painted a strong or intense color – or papered in a bold print – can serve to accentuate the way space is divided or provide a vibrant backdrop to a specific area within an open-concept space. A bright contemporary rug or a tiled floor can be a very

effective addition to a space where backgrounds are muted, as can glossy lacquered kitchen cabinets.

■ **Containment** Restricting the use of color or pattern to a single self-contained area is another option. You might wish to paint hallways and circulation areas in a strong shade, for example. This enlivens views and the experience of moving from area to area, without creating an overly dominant effect in main living areas. In much the same way, you can afford to be bolder with bathroom or cloakroom decorating, because such areas are not places where you spend a vast amount of time and neither are they open to the rest of the house.

If you are going to use strong color or overt patterning, allow plenty of breathing space so that the effect is not too overwhelming

3

2 The use of strong color can be surprisingly successful in hallways and staircases, where it has the effect of a vivid thread tying together different spaces in the home. This glossy red, which might be too dominant for a living area, adds a sense of vitality to those brief journeys up and down stairs.

3 Bright yellow combined with an orange-painted recess adds interest to a small bathroom. Fixtures are best kept white, as you do not want to have to change them when you tire of the color.

Color, Texture & Pattern

1 Pattern can be very effective displayed as a focal point on a single wall. Large-scale motifs often work better in small spaces than busy prints, which can seem claustrophobic.

2 Areas of pattern need plenty of breathing space. This stylized black and white floral design provides graphic interest in an otherwise all-white interior. The arrangement of decorative objects and pictures creates its own kind of pattern.

3 Strong warm colors, such as tones of orange and pink, generate a feeling of enclosure and intimacy that can be very appealing, even in spaces that are already restricted in size.

4 Big modernist prints are making a comeback. There is no need to wallpaper an entire room – panels and single sections of walls make ideal places for displaying pattern.

1

2

3

Decorating practicalities

Many decorating jobs are fairly straightforward, provided you follow some basic rules, prepare properly and use the right tools and materials. Others are largely professional jobs. Laying flooring, particularly heavy materials, tiling and installing worktops and other built-in features are generally best left to the experts.

Only you can decide how capable you are and how much time and effort you are prepared to devote to a given task. But it is important not to overestimate your abilities, especially if you have not tackled a particular job before. Tempting as it might be to save money by doing it yourself, if you make a mess of it, you'll either have to live with a substandard result or call in the professionals to fix your mistakes. It is bad enough paying for materials once – to pay twice because the job has to be done over again would be excruciating.

Preparation

Many decorating jobs – including painting – are nine-tenths preparation. What makes a good job is the work that goes on beforehand. If you are short on time and have given yourself a limited period to carry out the work, it can be very tempting to skip the preparation stage. This is a mistake. All surfaces need proper preparation for decorating; in a small space, imperfections will be all the more visible.

- Clear out as much as possible from the area you will be working on, including pictures, ornaments, furniture – anything that is easily moved. What you cannot remove, cover with dropsheets.

- Clean the area thoroughly, using a vacuum cleaner or brush. Wash surfaces with a proprietary cleanser to remove any grease and to provide a better surface for decoration.

- Cracks and shallow imperfections in the walls can be filled with drywall filler or spackling compound. You may need several applications; let the filler dry out and sand it smooth between each application.

- Fill any holes and cracks in the woodwork with

■ **Scale** Paradoxically, really big prints and motifs can be much more effective in small spaces than patterns that feature small repeats. Overscaled patterns have a tongue-in-cheek quality that serves to challenge spatial restrictions rather than acknowledge them.

Tempting as it might be to save money by doing it yourself, if you make a mess of it, you'll either have to live with a substandard result or call in the professionals to fix your mistakes

wood filler and sand smooth once it's dry. You may need several applications.

■ If wood or plaster moldings have become clogged with paint over the years, you will achieve the best result by stripping them. This is laborious and may involve many applications of a chemical stripper, but this is the only way to restore crispness of detail. Extremely clugged moldings may require professional restoration.

How to paint a room

■ First apply a layer of undercoater/sealer or primer to the walls and ceiling. You may need two coats if you are painting over a strong color.

■ Apply a top coat to the ceiling, working away from the main source of natural light.

■ Then apply a top coat to the walls, working away from the main source of natural light. Work in vertical strips from top to bottom.

■ Apply primer to woodwork – doors, baseboards and window frames. You may need two coats. Leave to dry completely, then lightly sand down before applying the second coat.

■ Apply the first coat to the woodwork. Higher sheen paints are recommended for woodwork because they are more durable than matte paints. Apply a second coat for durability even if color consistency appears to have been achieved.

■ Use a brush for painting woodwork and trim. You can use both a brush and a paint roller for walls and ceilings.

■ When painting walls, tape off all woodwork with painter's tape, and cut in all corners and trim with an angled sash brush. Fill in the rest of the wall with a roller appropriate for the sheen level of the paint. Always apply two coats.

Painting is a decorating job that is often done by DIY-ers, and the following tips should help you achieve a good result. Papering is more difficult than painting. Do not tackle it unless you are sure of your skills.

Lighting

Light and its partner, shadow, are the means by which space is revealed to us. Good lighting, both natural and artificial, is always important in the design of interiors, both practically and aesthetically. In small spaces it is crucial. A well-designed lighting scheme can go a long way to redress spatial limitations. The reverse is also true. You can plan and decorate your home with the utmost care, but without proper lighting the result will be sterile and charmless – and the space will appear even more cramped than before. Many people treat the whole issue of lighting as an afterthought, or certainly place it a long way down the list of priorities. This generally results in too much attention being paid to the style of fittings and lamps, and too little to the positioning, function and quality of the light they emit.

1 Imaginative use of lighting goes a long way toward creating atmosphere in the interior. Strip lighting concealed under the bed makes it appear to float over the floor and reduces the impact of what would otherwise be a dominant piece of furniture.

Lighting requires infrastructure – wiring, power outlets and switches. You may be in the fortunate position of having a system in place that will support your lighting requirements; more often than not, you will need to make changes or improvements, particularly if your property is old or is not a recent conversion. Because changes to lighting infrastructure are disruptive and involve channeling wires through walls, in ceiling voids or under floors, there is a sound argument for planning a lighting scheme in tandem with other spatial or decorating improvements. Once final finishes are in place, you will not want to disrupt them.

Points to consider

■ Planning a lighting scheme is greatly aided if you make use of a sketch or scale plan (see page 23). Study each area in your home at different times of the day – morning, noon, afternoon and evening – and note the basic orientation of natural light and its quality. Mark on any areas that are currently underlit, by both natural light and artificial light.

■ Think about work areas, such as kitchen counters, desks or any other part of your home where concentrated work is carried out. Are light levels sufficient for you to work safely and effectively? Are there obscuring shadows on the work surface? Kitchens require up to twice the level of lighting of general living areas; close desk work up to three times as much.

■ How flexible are the current lighting arrangements in the multipurpose spaces of your home? Would dimmer controls increase your options, both practically and aesthetically?

■ Are there enough switches and outlets in every area? Would it improve matters to install an additional lighting circuit so that you can control background light and local light independently?

■ What are the best features of your home? Does the present lighting arrangement emphasize these?

■ Are there trailing cords or overloaded outlets that might be a safety hazard? How recently has your wiring been updated? Electrical systems more than 15 or 20 years old require upgrading.

■ Think about any special conditions that might apply. Lighting in areas where there is the risk of water coming in contact with electricity needs to be carefully considered. Waterproof or sealed fixtures are essential, especially in small bathrooms and showers. Pay attention to safety in children's rooms: outlet covers and installed fixtrues well out of reach are advisable.

Lighting

Types of lighting

Before looking in detail at lighting schemes for small spaces, it is useful to gain an appreciation of the principal types of lighting and the various functions they serve. Many light fixtures are geared specifically for a single type of use; others are more multipurpose.

Most areas in the home require a combination of at least two different types of lighting:

Background or diffused light

Also known as ambient lighting, this type of light is essentially light to see by. Good background light should never be obvious but should remain in the background – glowing planes of walls or shaded lamps that create soft pools of light and shade are infinitely preferable to a single central light, which almost always results in a harsh, relentless atmosphere. Depending on the location, background light can be supplied by uplighters, downlighters, "wall-washers," sidelights and track lights, as well as floor and table lamps. For successful background lighting, the light must either be diffused in some way or the fixture concealed or recessed, so that it is light that you see, not lights. Dimmer controls allow you to adjust the light level – and mood – according to requirements.

1 A number of pendants are suspended over the length of a dining table at a height where they will not interfere with sightlines or cause glare.
2 Picking out a staircase using lights set into the treads, or at low level set into baseboards, creates a lit pathway of light that is very dramatic. Because the eye is led onward, the effect is to enhance the sense of space.

Floor-level spots, defining pathways or set into staircases or baseboards, add interest and definition to a lighting scheme

3 A contemporary standard lamp and a lit recess create diffused background lighting.
4 Concealing lighting behind panels at the gable end of this attic conversion brings out the character of the space. Lit, glowing edges accentuate architectural detail.

Directional light

Unlike background light, directional light is much more focused and provides a boost of illumination for a work area, where greater light levels are required, or to pick out a display, picture, detail or some other feature worthy of attention. Task lights include spotlights, adjustable track lights and desk lamps. Special picture lights and other lights designed for accenting decorative displays are also available.

Architectural lighting

Strip lights that are concealed beneath kitchen wall cabinets, under cornicing or plinths, or behind baffles have the effect of highlighting architectural detail or minimizing the bulk of built-in features and fixtures. Floor-level spots, defining pathways or set into staircases or baseboards, add interest and definition to a lighting scheme.

Information light

This type of light provides a low level of illumination in a very specific context. Examples include interior lights in closets and cabinets that are triggered by the opening of the door, lights over doorbells or keyholes, and lights in ovens and fridges – all situations where a small degree of local light is required to facilitate a specific task.

Decorative light

This final category comprises a range of sculptural and playful designs that serve very little practical purpose – and may not add very much in the way of overall illumination – but nevertheless contribute a certain beguiling charm. Simple strings of fairy lights, lit sculptures such as Tom Dixon's "Jack" light and colorwashing systems bring a new dimension into play. Firelight and candlelight also fall into this category but bring a mellow warmth to the room.

3

4

Lighting

Lighting schemes for small spaces

After you have completed the assessment of your needs, but before you commit yourself to a final choice of light fixtures, it is worth experimenting with different lighting arrangements. It is easier to do this with the help of a couple of friends or family members. You will need a ladder, a few extension cords and a number of basic lights, such as small table lamps, clip-on spots and so on. Pot lids or sheets of cardboard that you can use to vary the direction of the light are also useful.

■ Try out lights in different parts of the room, particularly corners that are presently underlit.
■ Vary the height of lights – lower down, midway and higher up.
■ Try out different combinations of wattages. If you increase the number of lights, you can afford to use lower-watt bulbs without reducing the overall light level.
■ Try bouncing light off walls and ceilings in different parts of the room to gauge the effect.

1 A cardinal rule of good lighting is to diffuse light sources wherever possible. A backlit glass shelf provides soft atmospheric light behind the headboard. An angled task light gives more concentrated focused light for reading.
2 Central or overhead lights should be avoided at all costs in bedrooms. They cause glare, which is tiring, and are overly dominant when viewed from a prone position. Here, light diffused behind a panel is warm and intimate.

Basic principles

■ **Avoid overhead or central lights** Never rely on a single central overhead light to deliver all the illumination in a given area. Single central lights cause glare, which is tiring and depressing; they also deaden the atmosphere and cast shadows into the corners, which makes rooms seem smaller. If you want a central light, choose a chandelier or a similar fixture that comprises many individual points of light and control it with a dimmer, so it is not overly dominant.

■ **Increase the number of light sources** Too few light sources inevitably causes glare. Even in a smallish living area,

you will need four to five different light sources. Vary their position and height to lead the eye through the space. Overlapping pools of light and shade will make a room seem bigger because everything is not uniformly lit.

■ **Target light at points of interest** Our eyes are naturally drawn to light. Make use of this by focusing light on whatever is worthy of attention – a fireplace, a decorative display or crisp architectural detailing.

■ **Limit the use of downlights** Downlights are not a universal lighting panacea. They are undoubtedly very useful in certain circumstances, such

as hallways or where there are fixed elements – in kitchens or bathrooms, for example. Elsewhere, they can be somewhat restrictive and even inhospitable.

■ **Bounce light off reflective surfaces** Direct light at the surfaces of walls and ceilings to create glowing backgrounds. Focusing light upward on the ceiling makes it seem higher; washing walls with light makes a room seem more spacious. This strategy is most successful when walls and ceilings are white or light in tone. Light diffused over walls and ceilings immediately enhances the sense of volume.

■ **Use architectural lighting** Many small spaces feature installed elements, such as built-in storage. Strip lighting concealed under such fixtures at floor level minimizes their bulk and makes them appear to float over the floor. Lights set at floor level accentuate the sense of progression from area to area.

■ **Install dimmers** Dimmers are essential in bedrooms and provide necessary flexibility in multipurpose spaces. In a kitchen/eating area you can turn the lights up to cook and prepare food, and down to provide a more welcoming atmosphere for dining.

2

Lighting

1 Uplighting is a good choice for small spaces, particularly those with low ceilings. Here, a light fixture angled upward bounces light off the upper portion of the walls as well as the ceiling, while concealed light is diffused through colored panels at low level.

2 Floor lamps are available in contemporary as well as traditional designs. This example has an articulated stem that allows you to vary the height of the light source according to need.

3 Gooseneck lamps and other types of task lighting are invaluable for providing a boost of concentrated illumination in work areas. Candlelight is immensely atmospheric.

4 Strip lights or tube lights concealed behind panels accentuate architectural detail. The effect will be particularly evocative if you use a colored tube or diffuse the light through a colored gel.

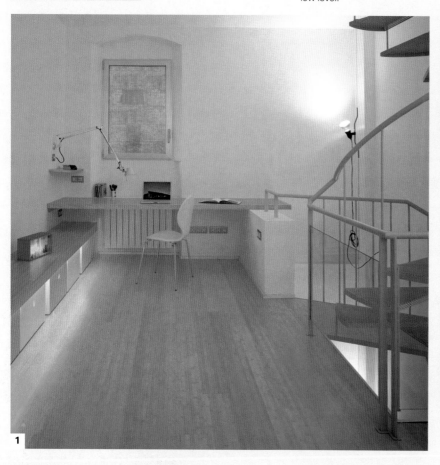

1

2

3

Choosing light fixtures

All too often, light fixtures are chosen on the basis of their appearance alone. While style is not irrelevant, it is much more important to consider the type of light that a fixture provides and whether that effect is appropriate for the particular context in which the light will be used. Always switch lights on before you purchase them. All fixed forms of lighting should be installed by a professional.

■ **Uplighters** These fittings, as the term suggests, target most of their light upward. Depending on the design of the fixture, the light spread might be fairly focused or more diffused. Uplighters make excellent fixtures for small spaces, especially where they are used to bounce light off the ceiling. Many uplighters are freestanding designs; some can be set into the floor; others are wall-mounted. In the case of wall-mounted designs, make sure these are not positioned too high up the wall, where their effect will be wasted.

■ **Downlights** Generally installed in position, either recessed into the ceiling or into the base of wall-hung units, downlights can be used to boost light levels in work areas or for more general illumination in areas where the layout is fixed. Small downlights can also be used to highlight display areas. Some designs are adjustable. Excessive reliance on downlighting, however, can limit your options for furniture arrangement unnecessarily.

■ **Wall lights** These are available in a wide range of designs, from traditional to contemporary. Less dominant than central fixtures, they often look best used in pairs, flanking a seating area, bed or chimney breast, for example. Some wall lights emit most of their light in one direction; others diffuse light through shades or globes.

Like the table lamp, the floor lamp is flexible, portable and versatile and has enjoyed something of a comeback in recent years

4

■ **Spots and tracks** There is a huge variety of spotlights and tracks on the market, from simple ceiling-mounted designs to bare-wire systems that allow individual lights to be positioned and adjusted as required. Spotlights vary in the width of their beam. "Wall-washers" direct a broad spread of light at the wall and create a diffused background light.

■ **Task lights** Practical lighting for work areas, particularly home offices and workshops, task lights often feature articulated arms to allow for easy positioning. The classic design is the gooseneck.

■ **Shadow lighting** This is hidden light coming from behind false walls, illuminating corners or ceilings.

■ **Table and floor lamps** The mainstay of home lighting is the table lamp, which comes in a vast choice of styles and price ranges. Most diffuse light through some sort of shade. Like the table lamp, the floor lamp is flexible, portable and versatile, and has enjoyed something of a comeback in recent years. Positioned around a room, floor lamps serve as spatial markers.

■ **Floor-level lights** A relatively new trend in domestic lighting schemes is to inset lights at floor level, either flush with the floor or stair treads, or recessed at the base of the wall. While such lights generally do not contribute a great deal to overall levels of illumination, the effect is very atmospheric.

■ **Hanging lights** Hanging, or pendant, fixtures – which range from the humble paper lantern to the chandelier – are best used either to light a dining table or to provide a gentle focal point in a living area. In neither case should they be the sole source of illumination – always combine hanging or central fixtures with other forms of local and background light.

Lighting

Choosing light sources

A light fixture controls the spread of light and determines whether it is directional or diffused. What makes the light, however, is the light source – the bulb, or "lamp," in technical terms. The most common domestic light source is the tungsten bulb. In recent years halogen bulbs have also become increasingly common, both in regular-voltage and low-voltage versions. Fluorescent bulbs, too, have improved considerably in terms of color and technical performance.

Tungsten

One of the most readily apparent differences between the various light sources is the color of the light they emit. Tungsten produces an intimate light with a warm, yellowish tinge that is both flattering and hospitable. It is the closest in tone to candlelight.

Advantages of tungsten
- Bulbs are cheap, readily available and easy to use.
- Tungsten bulbs run directly off electrical circuitry and are dimmable.
- Wattages range from 15 to 200 W.
- Lamps come in many different shapes and sizes to suit a wide variety of fittings, including globes, candle bulbs and tubes.
- Pearl, clear or tinted bulbs are available.

Disadvantages of tungsten
- Most of the energy that tungsten bulbs produce is converted to heat, which makes them both hot to touch and very energy-inefficient.
- Because they get so hot, they cannot be used close to flammable materials or in outdoor light fixtures.
- They have a very short lifespan compared to other types of light sources.

Halogen

Halogen's early uses were in retail displays, restaurants and other public contexts. The light emitted by this type of light source is much whiter and more sparkling than tungsten, and, as a consequence, closer to natural light in its rendering of color values. In the home, halogen is particularly useful in kitchens and other work areas where you need to make color judgments. Generally, this uplifting type of light works well in small spaces, particularly those decorated in white or light tones.

Advantages of regular-voltage halogen
- Like tungsten, bulbs respond immediately and are dimmable.
- Halogen lasts three times longer than tungsten.
- Wattages go up to 700 W.
- Bulbs are available as tubes or spots. Some incorporate dichroic reflectors.

Advantages of low-voltage halogen
- Bulbs are very small, so the fixtures can be very discreet.
- Light can be focused tightly on decorative displays.
- Bulbs are cooler and cheaper to run.
- Low-voltage halogen bulbs have a slightly longer lifespan than regular-voltage halogen.

Disadvantages of regular-voltage halogen
- It is not energy-efficient and generates considerable heat.
- Bulbs are more expensive and not as widely available.
- Fixtures must be heatproof and sited well away from flammable materials.

Disadvantages of low-voltage halogen
- You need a transformer to step the power down. Some are incorporated within the fixture; others require concealment, for example, in a ceiling void.
- Bulbs must not be touched with bare hands or grease will damage the quartz envelope.

Fiber optics and LEDs

Both fiber optics and LEDs (light-emitting diodes) can be used to make dramatic, even theatrical, lighting effects. Although both types of technology remain expensive and require specialized installation, their use may well become more widespread as prices fall. Because the light source is remote in the case of fiber optics, water can be lit safely. LEDs last an incredibly long time – between 50,000 and 100,000 hours.

Fluorescent

The fluorescent bulb has shed many of its dreary utilitarian qualities and found new domestic applications in recent years. In particular, improvements to color cast mean that the light emitted by these lamps is less greenish than it once was.

Advantages of fluorescent
- Bulbs are cheap and last eight times as long as tungsten.
- Bulbs come in a number of colors.
- They are very energy-efficient to run.
- Because bulbs generate very little heat, they can be used close to other materials and concealed behind baffles.
- Compact and mini-fluorescent bulbs now come with standard screw or bayonet caps, so they can be used in a wide range of light fixtures.

Disadvantages of fluorescent
- These bulbs, despite their improvements, do not render colors faithfully.
- They must be disposed of carefully because they contain toxic chemicals.
- Dimming is difficult without expensive equipment.
- Bulbs are not instantly responsive and may hum or flicker.
- Light levels gradually decrease over time.

1 Bulbs – or "lamps," as they are known in the lighting industry – come in a range of shapes to suit different fittings. As well as the standard household bulb (bayonet or screw), there are candle bulbs, spots of various sizes and linear tubes. Tubes can be fluorescent or tungsten.

Lighting

1 Extensive glasswork allows plenty of light into the interior, but it can cause uncomfortable extremes of temperature – too cold in winter, too hot in summer. One solution is to use low-E glass, which is highly insulating. Another option is to control the strength of natural light with slatted blinds. Filtering light in such a way also creates evocative shadow patterns.
2 Mirrors are an excellent way of enhancing the effect of natural light and increasing the sense of space. These folding mirrored closet doors reflect views internally and externally.
3 Skylights are inherently uplifting. Unlike windows in the wall surface, these openings frame only sky, which brings maximum light into the interior.

Natural light

Lighting schemes cannot be considered in isolation from conditions of natural light. As previously discussed, you can increase the amount of daylight that a room or area receives by a variety of alterations to the fabric of your home. These include adding new openings, increasing the size of existing ones and taking down internal partition walls so that light penetrates to otherwise underlit or dark areas (see pages 36–41).

If you are unable to undertake such improvements for any reason, or if existing natural light conditions are more or less adequate, it is still worth thinking about a number of other strategies that will enable you to make the most of what you have.

■ **Mirrors** Expanses of mirrors multiplies light and views. Walls opposite a window or doorway are ideal places to hang mirrors. Even windowless rooms, such as internal bathrooms, look bigger if you cover a substantial portion of one wall – or two facing walls – with mirror.

■ **Light-enhancing window treatments** Curtains or blinds that can be opened or raised up so the window is fully exposed make the most of available light. Extend rods or tracks well beyond the window frame on each side, or install blinds so they clear the frame at the top when they are raised. In some circumstances it can be worth installing blinds to the lower edge of the window frame so that they pull up over the lower half of the window. This allows natural light in from above while maintaining privacy.

■ **Filtering light** If windows need to be covered during the day for reasons of privacy – or to block out unlovely views – think about using some form of window treatment that will filter the light in interesting ways. Slatted blinds and panels of lacy semi-transparent fabric create patterns of light and shade that add vitality to the interior.

■ **Leave windows uncovered** Wherever possible, leave windows uncovered to make the most of available light. High-level windows rarely need any covering unless you need to block out strong sunlight to prevent heat levels rising unacceptably. Colored or obscured glass can provide an element of privacy without compromising existing light levels too drastically.

■ **Room allocation** If your home is arranged over several stories, it often makes sense to site bedrooms on the lower floor and living areas above, where the quality of light is better.

■ **Decor** As previously mentioned, using mainly light-toned decoration and reflective surfaces and finishes within a space will help spread the light around (see pages 56–61).

Furnishing Small Spaces

1 A clear floor and clean-lined architectural detailing provide an uncluttered background for furnishing. These simple pieces – a modern sofa bed, a couple of African stools, a butterfly chair and a glass-topped table – are modest and unassuming.

One of the most important ways of maintaining a sense of spaciousness is to keep the floor as clear as possible. While this obviously requires proper storage systems so that books and belongings are not sitting in heaps all over the place, it also means erring on the side of under, rather than overfurnishing. Freestanding pieces of furniture devour floor area, and may do so unnecessarily, without providing any great practical benefit. When your home is small, and especially if you are moving to a place that is smaller than your present accommodations, you need to accept that you will probably not be able to fit everything in. The first stage, therefore, is to assess what you really need and what you love; the second is to determine which space-saving strategy will work best for you.

1

■ If you are intending to buy a large piece of furniture, particularly a sofa or a bed, make sure you consult your scale drawings to ensure the item will actually fit in the allotted space – and, equally important, fit through the door. In some circumstances large pieces can be brought in through ground-floor windows, but that does not necessarily solve the problem if the eventual destination is up several flights of stairs and the landings are too narrow. If in doubt, take your drawings to the store and ask for advice.

■ Think about what you really need. One or two comfortable sofas may represent a better use of space than cluttering up the living room with armchairs, occasional chairs and side tables. Remember that you can always bring in extra seating from a dining area if you have an influx of visitors. Floor cushions and ottomans make good additional seating.

■ Opt for built-in storage as much as possible. Freestanding storage furniture is bulky and visually intrusive, and it creates dead space around it.

■ While some sofa designs, for example, are simply too big for a given space and appear too dominant as a consequence, it is not always successful to go to the other extreme and opt for really small-scale pieces, which may not provide the level of comfort you require and can give your home the look of a doll's house. In this context less is more, but smaller is not always the answer.

Multipurpose furniture
One way of minimizing the amount of furniture you require is to opt for multipurpose designs that serve more than one function. The sofa bed – and all its variants – is an obvious example. It is important to ensure such designs work equally well in both modes. A sofa bed that is neither a comfortable sofa nor a comfortable bed simply will not deliver what you need. Another point to consider is the ease of operation – if you put your back out every time you turn a sofa into a bed, or spend hours trying to reconfigure a pair of stools as a table, there is a serious shortfall of basic practicality. Many designers are experimenting with the potential of "transformable" designs. Some of the results are definitely more conceptual than helpful; others are positively ingenious. This sofa, called "Baby Elephant," features speakers built into two large adjustable "ears" on each side. It makes a dramatic alternative to going to a nightclub, as the base also vibrates when you turn up the volume.

Furnishing Small Spaces

Fold-down furniture and equipment

Aside from transformable designs – furniture that serves more than one function – other space-saving pieces include furniture that is built into the fabric of the room. The classic example is the wall bed, or Murphy bed, which folds down from the wall when in use and is stowed away again afterward. A related category comprises those types of furniture that are similarly easy to store when not required, such as stacking and folding chairs, tables and stools.

1 Fold-down tables As it is a flat surface, a table for dining or working can be readily folded back and secured to the wall when not required. There are a number of designs on the market, or you could commission a fold-down table from a skilled carpenter. Secure anchoring is essential.

Other space-saving tables:
- Gateleg or drop-leaf tables that can be opened out.
- Extending tables or tables with leaves.
- Tables with folding legs that can be stored when not in use.
- Stacking or nesting tables, chairs or stools for occasional use as the need arises.

One way of minimizing the amount of furniture you require is to opt for multipurpose designs that serve more than one function

2 Folding and stacking chairs If you live in a small space but like to entertain, folding chairs and stacking stools will enable you to accommodate guests from time to time without cluttering up your home with chairs you do not need on a daily basis. There is a wide range of designs available in metal, plastic, wood or a combination of materials; many are sold as garden furniture. The Alvar Aalto stacking stool is a contemporary classic that can serve many functions – as a seat, occasional table or bedside table – and be stacked away neatly in a corner when not in use.

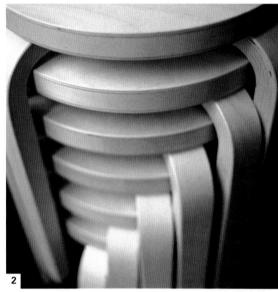

3 Other equipment Kitchens can be customized with fold-down or pull-out features to serve as additional counter space or work areas. Similarly, there are a number of space-saving ironing boards available, including those that simply fold away on piano hinges, drawer-mounted designs and ironing boards that fit into wall cabinets.

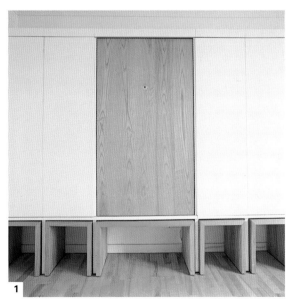

Furnishing Small Spaces

Space-saving beds

The ultimate in space-saving design, fold-down beds have been around for many years. Earlier examples were clumsy and unreliable in operation; today's designs are sophisticated and well engineered. Companies that supply folding beds generally provide an installation service. There is a wide range of styles and types available, including single, double and king sizes, fold-down bunk beds, revolving closet beds, sofa wall beds and desk-to-wall-bed conversions that enable you to use the space as a home office by day and a bedroom by night.

1 Contemporary wall beds come in every conceivable style, material and permutation. Size, too, varies, from widths of 3 ft. (0.9 m) to 5 ft. (1.5 m), and lengths up to 6½ ft. (2 m). Wall beds can be specified as part of a built-in storage unit, as shown in this example, where the bed slots into a framework of cupboards. Many wall beds come with the option of opening vertically or horizontally.
2 The great advantage of wall beds is that they allow a room to serve dual functions – living or work area by day, bedroom at night. As well as wall beds, there are even desk-to-bed conversions. Unlike old Murphy beds, where the bedding typically slid off when the bed was opened or closed, modern wall beds feature special fasteners to hold the bedding in place when the bed is not being used.

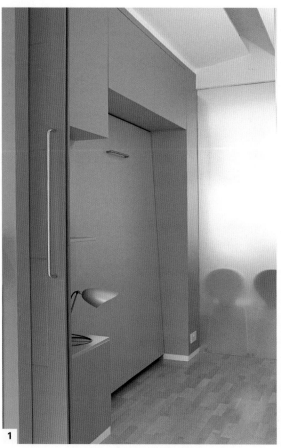

3 Another variation on the wall bed theme is bunk wall beds, which come complete with integral access ladder. These fold back against the wall into unobtrusive panels when not in use. Also on the market are sofas that convert into bunk beds with the operation of a single mechanism.

4 A "floor bed" rather than a wall bed, this mattress and platform slides out neatly from under a step to create an extra sleeping area in a multipurpose space. Some children's beds come with extra mattresses that slot in underneath – ideal for sleepovers.

Minimizing the impact of furniture

Even if space is very tight, most of us are going to need at least one or two larger pieces of furniture, items such as sofas, double beds and dining or work tables. While these do take up a considerable amount of floor area, there are ways in which you can minimize their visual impact. In addition, bear in mind that one floor finish throughout the room will also help give a sense of spaciousness.

■ **Alcoves** Position your furniture to make use of alcoves and recesses in order to keep the central area of the floor clear. Of course, alcoves are also ideal for the purposes of built-in storage, so you will have to weigh up the relative merits of each use.

■ **Long, low lines** Furniture that displays a strong horizontal emphasis will make an area seem more spacious, because what you lose in floor area will be offset by an increased sense of volume. Sofas with low backs, modular seating and floor-level beds are all designs suitable for this approach, which is particularly beneficial in rooms that have low ceilings, such as many attic conversions. Another advantage is that long, low lines instantly give a contemporary feel. By contrast, high-backed chairs and other types of furniture that have a strong vertical emphasis will naturally make a room feel more crowded. Remember that uncongested sightlines help give a sense of space.

■ **Simplicity of design** Avoid furniture with fussy detailing – choose sofas with straight or gently curved backs rather than elaborate scrolled contours; simple tables on basic supports or legs; basic divan beds.

■ **Transparency** See-through furniture includes glass tables, plexiglass chairs and seating that has an open wire framework. Garden furniture, designed to be light and portable, can work well in a small space.

1

1 A generous-sized seating area has been created in a bay window, with a long covered seat cushion and heaps of scatter cushions and pillows. A regular sofa of equivalent size would devour floor space – here the recess minimizes the impact. There is also room for storage underneath.

2 See-through furniture is naturally much less dominant. Glass-topped tables, plexiglass chairs and even garden furniture all work well in a small space.

■ **Understated upholstery** Any large upholstered piece, such as a sofa or easy chair, will be much less intrusive covered in white or a neutral fabric. Temporary cover-ups can be improvised by draping the piece in sheeting or a similar light material, or by opting for white loose covers in a washable fabric. The same goes for bed linen and bed covers.

■ **Sensitive lighting** It is best not to draw attention to large pieces of furniture by lighting them directly – for example, under a row of downlights – which will naturally bring them into greater prominence. Instead, position lights in the between-spaces, or so that light is reflected from walls and ceilings. Underlighting beds, bench seating and built-in storage makes such features seem less bulky and appear to float over the floor.

■ **Discreet heating** Underfloor heating may be expensive, but it frees up wall areas that might otherwise be given over to heat registers. Alternatively, opt for slimline radiators or wall registers to allow for a more flexible furniture arrangement.

Furnishing Small Spaces

Basic gear

Furnishing a home is not simply about making decisions about the big items, it is all the little stuff, too. The accessories of living range from cookware to cutlery (flatware), vases to fruit bowls, scissors to secateurs – incidental possessions that tend to multiply in many households. When you live in a small space, you need to rationalize these types of belongings to make the most of available storage and free up as much room as possible.

■ **Assess your needs** Only you can say if you could not be parted from your pasta maker at any cost. What is clear, however, is that if your kitchen is minute, you will have to curb your enthusiasm for acquiring gadget after gadget, giving houseroom only to those mechanical aids that really do save you time and reflect the way that you like to cook. Similarly, rent or borrow garden or do-it-yourself tools for those jobs you need to tackle only very rarely.

■ **Choose all-purpose gear** In the past most people kept two sets of dishes as a matter of course, using the "everyday" set for family meals and bringing out the "best" when they were entertaining. When you are living in a small space, you simply cannot afford to keep dishes on hand that make only occasional outings, and the same is true of glassware and cutlery (flatware). Instead, invest in simple products that are robust enough to stand daily use but handsome enough to grace your table, whatever the occasion. Similarly, good-quality casseroles and ovenproof dishes can be brought straight to the table – there is no need for separate serving dishes.

■ **Discard multiples** Possessions multiply for a variety of reasons. Sometimes we buy a replacement and hang on to the original item, just in case. Sometimes we buy a replacement for something that has been mislaid, but which later turns up. Often a couple who are setting up a home together for the first time

1

1 Choose glassware, cutlery (flatware) and dishes in simple classic designs that can be used both for entertaining and every day. Do not give houseroom to possessions that you will bring out only on Sundays and holidays.

2 Displays of favorite objects bring an interior to life and give it warmth and character. A backlit display shelf along one wall of a seating area provides a space to show off a collection of colorful pots.

find themselves with duplicate items. No one needs two can openers or six corkscrews. Choose the most efficient and discard the others.

■ **Minimal media** Now that flat-screen televisions have become more affordable and decent sound quality can be obtained from a pair of travel speakers hooked up to an MP3 player, media systems no longer have to dominate our living areas.

Details

There are two basic types of detail – those that are functional and those that contribute aesthetic pleasure of some sort, whether it is a jolt of color or a reminder of a pleasant occasion. While clutter, both visual and otherwise, rapidly undermines any sense of spaciousness, empty space can be rather sterile. You may have to be more selective about details in a small space, but you do not need to do without them entirely. Gather small items together and create a wall of texture, rather like a wall of books.

■ **Working details** Into this category fall doorknobs, handles and catches, handrails, balusters, blind pulls, switches and power outlets, and any other functional small-scale element that is designed to do a particular job. There are a number of ways in which you can treat such working details in a small space.

■ **Suppress or minimize** Many conventional details can be done without altogether if you are keen on a seamless look. Handles for cupboards and kitchen cabinets, for example, can be replaced by concealed chamfered fingerpulls or by press-catches. Clear plastic or glass switch plates interrupt the wall surface only minimally. While building codes say otherwise, many contemporary staircases have no handrails.

■ **Consistency** Stick to the same type of detail in the same material in every area of your home – if you have brushed-metal wall plates in the living area, for example, you should install the same in the bedroom.

This element of consistency is always important, but even more so in a small space.

■ **Quality** Decent handles and similar details can be surprisingly costly. An advantage of living in a small space is that you will need fewer of such items and therefore can afford to invest in high-quality designs.

■ **Displays** Every home, no matter how small, should provide room for those objects and pictures that give your life meaning and pleasure, otherwise you might as well be living in a hotel room. In fact, it is not unusual for those who travel frequently to pack a few items to make strange surroundings more hospitable – treasured photographs, a favorite throw or some other possession with sentimental value.

In a small space you need to give decorative displays plenty of breathing space. Group pictures on a single wall, rather than dot them about from place to place. Devote a single area to favorite decorative objects, rather than positioning them here and there. And, if at all possible, change displays from time to time, so that your eye always has something new to look at. Propped pictures are easier to move around than those that are hung on the wall.

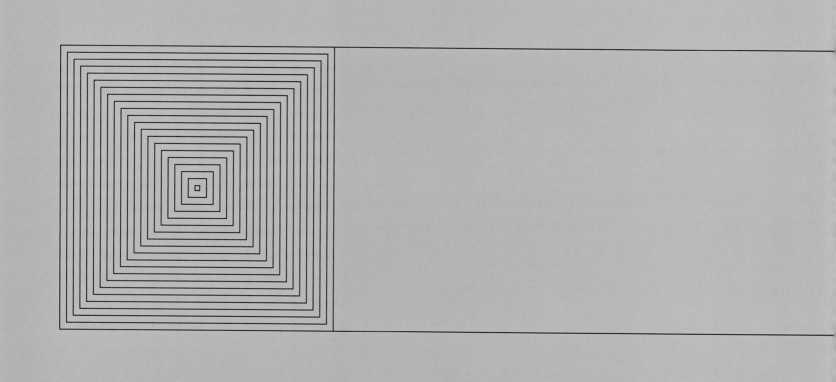

PART 1

MAKING THE MOST
OF SMALL SPACES

BRANCHING OUT

Getting the Work Done

The ultimate way to enhance a small space is to make it bigger physically. For work on this scale, as well as for many of the alterations detailed in the section "Design & Planning" (see pages 18–51), you will need outside assistance to get the work done to a proper standard. How much assistance, and of what type, will depend on the job in question. New additions, wherever they are sited, are major building projects and you will almost certainly need design and architectural advice, as well as the services of a number of professionals in various building trades.

1 Going up! A space that is subdivided vertically includes shelves for a CD collection and other possessions, a sleeping platform and cupboards in staggered levels up the stairs. Ingenious solutions often call for design input – consult an architect or interior designer.

Planning permits & legalities

Many types of alteration, particularly those that affect the external appearance of your home, require planning permission from your local building department. In most cases your plans must also conform to a number of other regulations concerning, for example, health and safety and fire escape routes. Generally, work will need to be inspected and passed at certain key stages.

Planning and building regulations vary depending on where you live; they are also subject to change, which makes it advisable to hire an architect or design professional to negotiate the bureaucratic hurdles on your behalf. Remember that if you steam ahead and do not apply for a permit for an alteration that requires it, the authorities can ask you to reverse the work (for example, take down the addition) at your own expense. Similarly, if you miss an inspection stage, you can be forced to retrace your steps so a proper inspection can be carried out – and this can be a very expensive, not to mention disheartening, experience.

Building codes and regulations

Any changes to your home that have structural implications – whether or not a permit is required (see right) – will have to be passed by a building inspector. There are also a number of other regulations concerning health and safety, drainage, fire protection and means of escape that will need to be met. While some of these regulations may seem petty, they are designed to protect the structural integrity of your property and that of your neighbors, and to keep you safe.

Do I need a permit?

In the case of major alterations, you will need to submit your outline proposals to your local planning department for consideration before the builders start work. This process allows for public consultation, which means your neighbors have the right to object if they think that what you propose to do will have an adverse impact on their lives. Many of the objections that are successfully upheld concern additions or alterations that block natural light in a neighboring property. You will likely need a permit for the following spatial changes but check with your planning department to be on the safe side:

■ Converting a building, portion of a building or outbuilding from industrial or commercial use into residential accommodation.
■ Building onto party walls shared with neighbors.
■ Extending at ground level beyond a specified distance, above a specified height or in such a way as to increase the cubic capacity of your home by more than 10 percent.
■ Changing the shape of your roof.
■ Splitting your home into two dwellings.
■ Installing a dormer in the front or side of your home.
■ Building an additional story onto the top of the main building or onto the top of an existing addition.
■ Altering a listed historical building or one that is situated in an historical area.

Hiring professionals

For the type of alterations detailed in this section, you will almost certainly need professional help. Such assistance falls into five main categories: design and advisory services; specification and sourcing; supervisory services; building work; and specialized services. The more complex the job, the more likely it is that you will require assistance from professionals in each of these categories.

Design and advisory services

■ **Architects** As all-round design specialists, architects provide an invaluable service when it comes to exploring potential options for improvement, alteration and extension. An architect will work with you to come up with a plan that delivers what you want within your financial means, as well as within practical, legal and planning parameters. You can hire an architect to oversee a job from start to finish, or simply engage his or her services until the proposed plan has gained planning permission.

■ **Structural engineers and surveyors** You (or your architect) may need to consult a structural engineer or surveyor if there are structural defects in your property, complicated structural issues to resolve with respect to your proposals or issues relating to neighboring properties.

■ **Interior designers or decorators** While building work and any related structural issues are largely out of their range, interior designers can provide invaluable advice on materials, furnishings and decorating schemes.

■ **Specialized design services** Many manufacturers of kitchens, bathrooms and built-in storage provide in-house design advice. Some companies specialize in a particular type of alteration, such as attic or basement conversions, and these, too, provide design advice and may also be able to negotiate the relevant permissions for you.

1

1 An additon into a side passage creates a new kitchen area with a sloping glass roof. Curtains are ideal for screening space – make sure they are weighted in the hem so they hang properly. This curtain can be drawn across to hide the kitchen from the dining area.

Specification and sourcing

A detailed, written specification translates your wishes into concrete choices with respect to materials, detailing and fixtures. If you have hired an architect to oversee the plan, they will be able to prepare a specification on your behalf that fits with your preferences. Otherwise, you will have to make what you want clear to builders and other tradespeople. Do not be vague or ambiguous: left to their own devices, builders will choose the cheapest and easiest option, which may not be what you want and may cost more than it's worth.

Supervisory services

Making sure everything happens in the correct order, that deliveries are made on time and tradespeople turn up when they should, makes all the difference between a job that is completed on schedule and within budget and the nightmare scenario of delay and cost overrun. If the job is relatively straightforward, you may wish to undertake this role yourself – but you need to be informed about the sequence of work (see pages 94–5). Otherwise, you can hire an architect to carry out regular site supervision and make sure the work is done to a proper standard and all necessary inspections are made at the correct time. Failing that, a building contractor will be able to coordinate work on site, but you need to be sure the firm has a good track record in this respect.

Making sure everything happens in the right order and on time makes all the difference between a job that is completed on schedule and within budget and the nightmare of delay and cost overrun

Building work

There are two basic routes when it comes to getting the job done. Either you can hire tradespeople directly – which is advisable only if the work is simple – or you can engage a contractor. Building contractors tend to keep only a few workers on their books, hiring more specialized services on a subcontract basis. A good contractor will undertake site supervision, arrange deliveries and generally coordinate every aspect of the work at hand.

Specialized services

Most jobs require specialized services as well as general construction work. These include:

- **Scaffolders**
- **Installers** For example, carpet or other flooring installers
- **Roofers**
- **Plumbers**
- **Electricians**

Employing others

■ The best recommendation is often word of mouth. Ask friends who have had similar work done.

■ All professionals should be members of an accredited body or trade organization. This gives you redress in case of dispute.

■ Collect references and ask to see examples of previous work (this is especially relevant when choosing an architect).

■ For large jobs, draw up a shortlist of three firms and ask for estimates.

■ Put everything in writing. Standard building contracts are available that allow you to agree on terms of payment, start and completion dates, and full specification of works.

■ Never pay up front. For small jobs, an amount can be paid at the start as a down payment. For larger jobs, you may wish to agree to a weekly or biweekly schedule. In either case, retain a significant proportion as a final payment to ensure satisfactory completion. It is better to agree on a flat contract sum than to arrange payment on an hourly or day rate. ALWAYS include a percentage (say 10 to 15 percent) that you retain as a contingency allowance in case things go wrong.

Getting the Work Done

Managing the work sequence

Even if you do not intend to take on a supervisory role yourself, it is still important to be aware of the likely sequence of events. Some jobs are inevitably more complicated than others and may require official inspections at certain key stages. If you know what should be happening at any given time, you may be able to avoid holdups and unnecessary delays.

In most jobs, bar the simplest, there is an element of toing and froing, which means different trades have to work around each other. For example, the plumber will be involved at an early stage, laying service connections and pipework, and then return, somewhat later, once walls are in, to install sinks and bathtubs. This means that every person involved in the job has to keep to his or her own allotted place in the puzzle. Once you factor into the equation deliveries of fixtures and materials, you can see how complex matters can become. Depending on the job, some or all of the procedures outlined on the right may be required.

If you know what should be happening at any given time, you may be able to avoid hold-ups and unnecessary delays

On site

■ Allow reasonable access to kitchen and toilet facilities.

■ Do not interfere with the proceedings unnecessarily. Be on hand to inspect work at the end of the day and discuss any issues that might require a decision. Otherwise, keep out of the way.

■ Try to refrain from changing your mind about design or specifications once work has begun. Too many alterations to work in progress causes delays, increases costs and means frustration for your builder and architect.

■ Agree on rules about working practices – for example, where tools and materials are to be stored and the degree of tidiness and cleanliness you expect.

■ Plan ahead so you have alternative arrangements in place for those periods when services will be interrupted or work that is very messy, noisy or disruptive will take place.

1 Permits Do not proceed without the necessary permits in place. If the plan entails alterations to services, you need to contact the relevant utility well before your start date.

2 Demolition and site preparation Removing unwanted structures, erecting scaffolding, clearin furniture, protecting existing surfaces, demolishing walls and internal partitions, removing drywall.

6 Ground-floor construction Another inspection stage, this entails the construction of the ground floor structure, which in some cases is a concrete slab.

7 Shell or superstructure You will now see real progress as the shell of your addition goes up anc the roof is covered.

11 Exterior doors and windows Doors and windows are leveled and installed.

12 First-fix Constructing staircases, routing wiring and plumbling internally, installing heating, covering walls with drywall.

If things go wrong

■ Do not panic. If you have included a contingency in your budget, you should be covered. But do be prepared, because most jobs throw out something unexpected along the way.

■ Think laterally. If a certain material you have specified is suddenly unobtainable or a supplier goes out of business, you should be able to source an acceptable alternative that performs the job equally well.

■ Be understanding. Bad weather or unforeseen structural defects can cause unavoidable delays and unexpected expense. Neither of these are the fault of your builder or architect.

■ Put all complaints in writing. Sit down and try to resolve issues amicably. Often there is fault on both sides. Good communication is essential.

■ If all else fails, take up the dispute with a relevant professional a body.

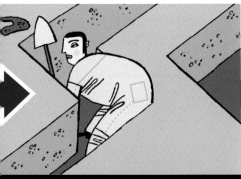

3 Excavations Extensions will require trenches to be dug for foundations and service connections. This age may be held up oweing to bad weather.

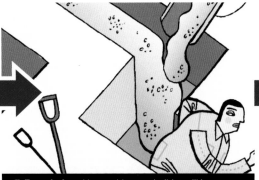

4 Foundations Your architect or builder will have specified the type of foundations required. Once these have been laid, they will need to be passed by the building inspector. Again, bad weather can cause delay.

5 Waterproofing and foundation brickwork After the foundations are laid, the next stage is to build up to ground level (in brick or blockwork). Then the waterproofing is done. This work requires inspection.

8 First-fix carpentry Work on door and window frames, installing exterior doors, making stud partitions, adding floor joists.

9 Drains and services Laying pipework for new drains and making external connections to electricity, gas and telephone. Trenches must not be covered up until drains are tested and passed and connections inspected.

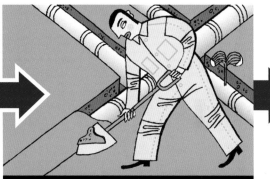

10 Filling in drainage and service trenches Once the previous stage has been inspected and passed by the relevant authorities, the trenches can be filled in.

13 Second-fix Installing toilets, sinks, switches, lights, heat registers and power outlets. Interior doors, woodwork, built-in storage and the installation of kitchen and bathroom cabinets.

14 Decorating Tiling, painting and general decorating, final floor finishes.

15 Final inspection and handover The building inspector makes a final inspection. If you have hired an architect, he or she will inspect the work for any defects.

Converting Attics

One of the most popular of all home improvements, attic conversions add space, value and character to your home. They are also easier to carry out than many other forms of conversion or extension, and generally less contentious in planning terms (see "Permits and regulations" on page 98).

Simple conversions can be carried out yourself or by using the services of a building company specializing in this type of work. If you require more than a basic conversion, particularly if you will be using part of the space as a bathroom, for example, it is generally best to consult an architect.

1 Open to the eaves. The exposed rafters and beams in this barn conversion give a great sense of character to the loft level.

■ Think about how you will want to use the additional space. You may have decided to convert your attic because you need another bedroom, for example, but that does not necessarily mean you have to use the new area for that purpose. Look at the way rooms or areas are allocated throughout your home. Using an attic as a dedicated work area might free up another room that is currently serving as your study on a more accessible level.

■ Converted attics are cozy and intimate, which makes them natural retreats. Because they offer a degree of separation from the rest of the household, they make good spaces for renters or semi-detached family members (older teenagers or live-in students, for example), as well as for private work areas.

■ Roof windows provide a good quality of natural light, which can be beneficial for concentrated work. If the rest of your home is poorly lit, consider floor-level glass in the new area or a generous open stairwell to draw light down to the areas below.

■ If you need to replace or renew your roof, think about converting your attic at the same time, even if you have no present use for it. A basic conversion, which includes the installation of skylights or a dormer and the strengthening and boarding out of the floor, can always be upgraded with final finishes later. Combining roof repair and attic conversion makes financial sense because up-and-over scaffolding, which major roof overhauls require, accounts for a considerable proportion of the expense of both types of work.

■ Even if your attic does not provide enough floor area – or enough floor area at the required head height – to serve as a habitable room, you might consider installing skylights and removing a portion of the attic floor in order to enhance the overall sense of volume on the level below.

■ Consider using your attic space for storage, as this can free up space in the rest of the house.

Converting Attics

Permits and regulations

There are a number of rules and regulations that govern attic conversions. While many attic conversions do not require planning permission, always err on the cautious side and seek advice as to whether what you are proposing to do is acceptable.

Points to consider

■ In some areas, regulations stipulate that at least half of the floor area in the converted space must have minimum head room of 7½ft. (2.3 m). Adding a dormer will increase available head room and hence usable floor area. If this does not increase head room by the required amount, your only other option would be to lower the floor, which complicates the building work considerably and may adversely affect rooms on the level below.

■ You do not need a permit if you are simply installing skylights in the roof and are not altering the shape of the roof in any way.

■ Dormer windows must be no larger than a specified size. Generally, rear dormers do not require permits; those at the front or side, or those that look out over a public space, do require permits.

■ All attic conversions in historic areas require permits.

■ All structural work to the roof or the floor must be approved by a building inspector.

■ You will need to seek a party wall agreement with your neighbors if the conversion entails building onto a party wall.

■ Fire regulations come into play if your home has more than two storie. You may need to install a fire door to separate the new area from the rest of the household. Regulations regarding means of escape may affect the design and siting of access stairs.

1

Options include skylights, which sit flush with the roof, and dormer windows, which increase usable floor area. Think about basic practicality. At least some of the windows must be openable to ventilate the space – heat rises and roof spaces can become very warm. Designs that pivot allow for ease of cleaning – there is nothing worse than gazing up at a view of the sky through a dirty pane of glass. Many skylights incorporate integral blinds that let you vary light levels.

1 Opening up into the roof allows you to position skylights over the stairs, where they will spill light down to lower levels. This attic conversion provides much-needed space for a home office.
2 This attic has been converted to provide a bedroom and bathroom. To make the most of natural light, a glass walkway links the open stairwell with the two new rooms. A skylight positioned directly above the glass floor draws light down into the lower levels.

2

Converting Attics

1 Attic conversions can improve spatial quality on the levels below. Absorbing the roof void creates a high-ceilinged living space flooded with natural light. Here, the stairs lead to a roof deck.
2 Converted attics are ideal for bedrooms, as they are tucked away at the top of the house out of main traffic routes. Positioning the bed against the end wall is a good use of available space.

Structural issues

Whether or not an attic conversion is feasible will be determined first and foremost by the roof structure itself. Older properties generally present few problems in this respect. New homes, however, often have preformed roof trusses, which means that conversion of the attic space will be near impossible.

In general, however, building work is fairly straightforward. The main structural work consists of strengthening floor joists – the joists in an attic are not as strong as those on lower levels – and strengthening the roof structure to support the weight of roof windows. In both cases joists and rafters are braced by bolting on additional supports alongside existing ones. If you are installing a dormer, the roof structure will also require additional support over the new opening.

Whatever additional work is required will depend both on the existing arrangements and on how you intend to use the space. It might be necessary, for example, to move a chimney stack . There may also be changes to electricity, heating and possibly water and drainage.

Whatever additional work is required will depend on both the existing arrangements and how you intend to use the space

1

Access

Most unconverted roof spaces are accessed from the level below via a hatch in the ceiling, which may or may not be fitted with a retractable ladder. Converted attics, however, generally require a more permanent and stable arrangement. Which solution you adopt will to some extent depend on how frequently you will need to access the attic space, as well as available floor area.

If you will be using the attic only intermittently, upgrading to a strong attic ladder that can be folded away into the roof space will usually be adequate. You may need to enlarge the hatch opening to accommodate the ladder and to allow bulkier items of furniture to be moved into the attic.

Daily or regular use requires a more permanent solution. You can opt for a spiral staircase, a permanently secured ladder or one of the space-saving staircase designs featured on pages 46–7. These solutions, however, are not particularly advisable if the converted attic is intended to provide accommodation for young children or the elderly.

The most comfortable, flexible and safe option is to provide access via a new staircase. However, this solution does result in the loss of a degree of floor area in the level below and it may necessitate changes to the layout.

If your home is arranged over two stories, fire regulations may stipulate that access to the new area should be via a closed fire-protected staircase.

2

Converting Attics

Design

Attic spaces, thanks to the sloping planes of the roof, have immense character and charm. When it comes to designing and decorating an attic, it is well worth opting for solutions that enhance the quirkiness of the space. As it is a self-contained area at the top of the house, there is no particular need to restrict yourself to the same palette of surfaces and finishes used elsewhere in your home.

1 Under the eaves
The area under the eaves, where the roof slopes down to meet the floor, is a natural place for built-in storage. A row of seamless cupboards, pull-out bins or drawers on casters, or even a neat array of uniform containers can accommodate a considerable amount of possessions – serving as storage for work supplies or clothing, or deep repositories for items not in frequent use. In some attics, where the roof rests on a supporting wall, there may be enough head room for you to position a desk or a bed in this area.

Most converted attics do not see a great deal of traffic, so flooring materials do not need to be as durable as they do in a kitchen or living area

2 Surfaces and finishes

As is the case with other small spaces, a light and airy decorating palette will enhance the sense of spaciousness. White and other pale shades work particularly well in areas where natural light is coming from above. Variety can be introduced with contrasts in texture. You may wish, for example, to leave brickwork exposed on a gable end or to finish roof beams and rafters in a natural seal. Tongue-and-groove paneling is another good material choice and looks particularly crisp painted white. The ceiling will probably need to be insulated.

3 Low-level living

Most converted attics have less head room than standard rooms, which can be somewhat claustrophobic. Low-level furniture – such as mattresses laid directly on the floor or on low bedframes, floor cushions and low tables – can help mitigate the sense of restricted volume.

3

4

4 Flooring

There are several practical considerations to take into account when choosing flooring for a converted attic. A key factor is sound. Hard or wooden surfaces will transmit impact sound – footsteps, for example – very readily to rooms or areas on the level below. If you wish to rent out your attic, you will need to lay a sound-insulating subfloor to keep noise within an acceptable level. You should also bear in mind that, even when attic joists are doubled up, the resulting floor is generally not strong enough to take the heavier flooring materials, such as stone and tile. However, most converted attics do not see a great deal of traffic, so flooring materials do not need to be as durable as they do in a kitchen or living area, for example.

Good flooring choices:
- Carpeting laid over a good-quality underlay.
- Natural-fiber coverings – for example, sisal, seagrass, coir or jute – laid over a good-quality underlay.
- Wood floors, provided they are laid over sound insulation.
- Plywood sheets, provided they are laid over sound insulation.

Converting Basements

In many parts of the world where both old and new houses include a full-height basement as a matter of course, the usefulness of this extra level below ground has long been recognized. Until relatively recently, however, cost and difficulty meant that basement conversions were something of a rarity. That has now changed. While converting a basement remains expensive and can involve more extensive and complex building work than an attic conversion, improved building techniques, combined with high property prices and sheer pressure on space, have seen this form of home improvement become much more popular. Proof of this can be gauged by the number of new companies specializing in basement and cellar conversions.

1 Basement areas can have plenty of charm and character, provided they are well lit. While these conversions do tend to be more expensive and disruptive, the gain in space can make them cost-effective in the end.

Basements, like attics, have traditionally served as utility areas – places where washing machines, freezers and other bulky and noisy appliances are located, along with space-devouring possessions, such as sports equipment and household files. Outfitted to a minimal standard, they have also been pressed into service as children's play areas.

Nowadays space is simply too valuable in many areas and the price of moving so high that basement conversions are looking much more cost-effective. Existing basements are being upgraded into living areas and new basements dug out under existing foundations to extend space downward. With inspired, innovative design, such below-ground spaces can be surprisingly light and add an entire level of floor space to your home, without the restricted head room offered by attic conversions.

The options

■ **Converting an existing basement** If you have an existing basement with enough head room, building work is generally fairly simple and may be restricted only to improving stairs, installing plumbing and electrical, if necessary, and installing ground-level openings to draw natural light down into the space. The remainder of the work will consist of water-proofing and installing proper wall and floor finishes.

■ **Converting a semi-basement** Semi-basements on a sloping site offer the most potential. You may need to excavate adjacent garden areas to improve access and natural lighting. Waterproofing will also be required. Old coal cellars, storm cellars and root cellars can also be enlarged and converted.

■ **Creating a new basement** The most expensive and disruptive option is to excavate under your home to create a new basement level. An alternative, which is cheaper and less complex, is to create a new basement immediately adjoining your home and extend over the top of it.

Converting Basements

1 Glossy white finishes make the most of available light in this basement conversion. Even the balustrade is see-through, to draw light down from the upper level.
2 One way of bringing light into the basement is to excavate a portion of the ground immediately adjacent to it, in order to form an overscaled lightwell. The effect here has been accentuated by roofing the basement addition in glass.

1

Permits

Most basement conversions require planning permission. Any conversion, for example, that involves the creation of a lightwell or that is intended to be used as a habitable room will need approval. If work will involve altering or building onto party walls, you will also need to get an agreement from your neighbors. If the work involves underpinning, you will need architect's drawings and calculations from a structural engineer. Fire escapes can also be an issue and will need to be inspected by a building inspector. If drainage has to be rerouted, you may need advice and permission from your utility company.

Waterproofing

As underground spaces, basements naturally tend to be a bit damp. Whether you are converting an existing basement or creating a new one, full waterproofing will need to be carried out. This can be achieved by "tanking," or rendering surfaces with an impermeable layer, by installing a waterproof membrane or by constructing walls and floor from waterproof materials. There are also sophisticated modern systems of waterproofing that control water rather than exclude it. These combine waterproof construction and moisture-proof membranes with drainage channels and pumps, to extract and reroute ground water. Dry-lining systems are applied over the waterproof membrane.

Structural issues and building work

While creating a new basement is rarely impossible, some projects are more difficult than others. A key consideration is ground conditions. You (or your architect or engineer) will probably need to conduct a soil survey to establish what type of foundations will be required. Tree roots may also pose a problem.

Then it is a question of existing foundations. In older properties without basements, the ground floor is usually suspended over a shallow void, the floor joists resting directly on foundation walls. To create a new area with sufficient head room – 7 ft. 8 in. (2.4 m) is the recommended minimum – the ground will have to be dug out and the existing foundations underpinned with concrete. The same holds in properties where the floor rests directly on the ground – where it is a concrete slab, for example. In both cases, creating a new basement will put the ground floor out of commission for more or less the duration of the job. An advantage of creating a new basement as an extension of your property, siting it in a front or back yard, for example, is that such disruption is minimized, but it will undoubtedly improve on your life in the house.

Converting Basements

Natural light

One of the most crucial elements in basement conversions is ensuring the space is adequately lit by natural daylight. Depending on site, structure and context, there are a number of ways by which this can be achieved.

- **Lightwell** By extending a little way out into the yard, you can create a lightwell that brings natural light down from above.
- **Glass roof** Extending semi-basements further into the yard offers the opportunity to glaze the roof of the basement conversion.
- **Enlarging or increasing existing openings** This is the most obvious way to increase natural light levels.
- **Adding glass panels in the floor above** As with a glass roof, glass panels in the basement ceiling will draw light down from the area above.
- **Creating an open-concept space** Removing any interior partition walls in an existing basement and decorating the space in light colors and finishes will spread the available light around as much as possible.

Potential uses

Modern building and drainage techniques mean there are few restrictions with respect to potential uses of basements. A converted basement may be used as a kitchen, a bedroom and bathroom, a playroom, or even as a self-contained apartment. At the upper end of the market, converted basements have been used to provide luxury facilities – pools, Jacuzzis, gyms, home cinemas and wine cellars – a far cry from the damp, dark, cobwebby spaces of popular imagination.

1

Because basements are dug out of the earth, they retain heat for longer and lose it more slowly than upper levels where external walls are exposed

2

1 Reflective steel finishes combined with glass stair treads and walkways enhance natural light in this basement kitchen. Nowadays, drainage techniques have improved dramatically and there are few limits to the uses to which a converted basement can be put.

2 An extensive glass panel in the floor above lights a basement living area. The all-white decoration and pale wood floor dispels any hint of gloominess.

Cost-effectiveness

Excavation – using small diggers – underpinning and other related structural issues do mean basement conversions are more expensive than other types of home alteration – between twice and four times the cost of an attic conversion, for example. The net gain, however, will be to increase the size of your home dramatically. If you consider the present value of your home and divide it by existing floor area, you can compare the cost of the alteration with what your home will eventually be worth once the conversion has been carried out.

Then there are the savings, both environmental and economic, to be made through increased energy efficiency and minimal land use. Because basements are dug out of the earth – literally earth-sheltered – they retain heat for longer and lose it more slowly than upper levels where external walls are exposed. A house with a basement is 10 percent more energy-efficient than a house of a comparable size and construction that does not have one. Many government agencies and local authorities are keen to promote the provision of basements in new developments for this reason, and also because they provide additional living space without losing more land to construction. Always check that your existing heating and power installation can cope with the extension of space.

Additions

One of the most complex of all home improvements, putting on an addition potentially pays off the most, in both spatial and financial terms. In many instances, an addition is more cost-effective than moving to a larger property and it will certainly add value to your home. The scale of such projects, their expense and their impact on the rest of your home mean professional design advice is almost always necessary, at least until you get the necessary permits.

1 This radical design for an addition to a Georgian house came about when local planners stipulated that any windows must match the 18th-century originals. The architect, Henning Stummel, while prepared to use traditional materials, drew the line at pastiche. As the extension houses two bathrooms on two separate levels, and bathrooms do not have to have windows, his solution was to use sanded plexiglass boards to let in the light. By day these blend in with the exterior's gray-painted cladding; at night they glow.

■ Think hard about what you require in terms of additional space before you hire an architect, designer or builder. At the same time, keep an open mind about how these needs may best be met. During initial consultations, a design professional will be able to look at your home as a whole and possibly suggest alterations to existing layouts that will make the most of what you have, as well as coming up with ideas for the new addition. Most successful additions do not simply consist of additional space bolted on, but are fully integrated with existing areas; in some cases transforming them in the process.

■ Where are you feeling the pinch? In some cases it is pretty straightforward – there is a new addition to the family and another bedroom is urgently needed.

■ In which part of your home would you most welcome extra room – in general living areas? In the kitchen?

■ Is there any activity or function that is critical to you but which your home cannot accommodate? A shift from an office job to home-based work, for example, will pose additional demands on space and the need for some separation between home and working life.

■ Are there any areas in your home that have little natural light? Could an addition improve matters, or would you be at risk of darkening existing spaces?

■ What impact would the addition have on the way you currently use different areas in your home? A fully inclusive new kitchen, for example, might well become the focus of family life, rendering existing living areas more or less redundant.

■ Which aspects of your home give you the most pleasure? An addition should represent a direct improvement, not compromise what you already have.

■ As creating an addition involves a considerable degree of building work, it might be cost-effective to combine such a project with other improvements to your home. That way, you only have builders in once.

■ A shed in the yard may be the most economical and least disruptive solution.

Additions

1 Two intersecting boxes create a two-story addition to an Edwardian home. The windows are designed around the views, with the large picture window at the upper level providing a view of the city and the narrow openings at the lower level looking out over the yard. The addition has a softwood frame and black-stained wood cladding. **2** "Hut-on-a-roof" is a kitchen on a London rooftop. It features a sliding glass roof and wood-burning stove and is insulated with sheep's wool. **3** A simple metal-framed glass structure makes an atmospheric rooftop bathroom.

Siting

One of the key factors in planning an addition is deciding where it should be sited. You may, of course, have little choice, and local restrictions and structural considerations may limit your options further. There may be solutions you have not considered – side infills, for example, are often overlooked in favor of rear additions, but can be surprisingly effective.

Options

The most common type of addition is to the rear at ground level. Sunrooms, garden rooms and extended kitchen/dining areas offer the opportunity to connect your home with outdoor spaces. Because such extensions are screened from the street, they can feature expanses of glass without loss of privacy. The trade-off, however, is that you will have to sacrifice some of your yard, unless there are existing sheds or outbuildings that can be demolished to provide space for the addition.

Side additions range between new wings built on land at the side of your property to side infills incorporating existing passages or narrow strips of yard between your home and the property line. In semi-detached or townhouse properties, the side or rear "return" may appear quite minimal, but the addition of even such a relatively small space can transform ground floors, especially if the addition features top lighting or a glazed roof. In some contexts side additions can range over two or more stories.

Building over an existing addition is also a possibility. If there is a window at the upper level, you may be able to enlarge this opening to create a doorway that connects to the new addition.

Rooftop additions have the potential to increase your home by an entire story and to bring top lighting down into internal areas. You may also be able to take the opportunity to create a roof deck or outdoor living space.

Prefab extensions

Most people are familiar with the "bolt-on" sunroom, generally available in kit form for rapid construction, and often rather dreary in style and appearance. Today, however, some companies are producing prefab additions to customers' individual specifications, which broadens the design scope considerably.

This type of addition is constructed in a factory, either as a complete unit or as a kit of parts; after delivery to site, it can be ready for occupation in a matter of days, once basic service connections have been made.

Additions

1 When you are siting and designing an addition, it is important to consider the new spatial relationships within the house and with respect to outdoor areas. This dining room addition has sliding glass doors onto a patio. The white garden wall helps extend the interior space visually.

Permits

Most additions have considerably more impact on neighbors and the local environment than attic or basement conversions, where the work is largely internal. Building work is always unavoidably noisy and disruptive – when it is taking place in the open air, the sound is magnified and the nuisance multiplied. Whereas you can comfort yourself with the thought of how wonderful it is going to be when the addition is finally completed and you are able to enjoy your spacious new home, your neighbors will suffer the annoyance during the construction period without reaping any benefits at the end of it. Even if your addition does not require planning permits or a party wall agreement, it is only common courtesy to explain your plans at the outset and outline how long the work is expected to take. You may also wish to inform them when deliveries of materials are likely to take place or when any other stage in the proceedings that is potentially disruptive is about to occur.

If your plans do require permits, it is a good idea to talk them over with your neighbors before you submit your proposals to the planning department – or have your architect do so on your behalf. Neighbors often challenge plans because they do not fully understand them – and fear the worst. You can save yourself a great deal of time by putting their minds at ease right at the start.

Permits are not always required for small single-story rear additions, provided that the addition is under a certain height, is within a given distance of the property line and does not increase the cubic content (or volume) of your home by more than 10 percent. However, check with your local planning department to make sure.

Additions that increase your home by more than 10 percent need planning permits, as do those over two or more stories or those that back onto party walls shared with your neighbors, in which case you will also need a signed agreement from your neighbors. Roof pitches can be critical in gaining approval. If your plan would block natural light from a neighbor's property, it may well be turned down.

Additions that affect the way your property appears from the street also require planning permits. Roof extensions may be ruled out altogether in historic areas or in streets where houses all have the same number of stories.

The new addition will also have to comply with building regulations and work must be inspected at certain key stages. These include the construction of foundations, the laying of drains and the erection of the principal structure. Fire codes and other safety legislation must also be met.

A new addition must be insulated to current standards laid down in building codes, even though these may not be met in your existing property.

It is a good idea to talk over the plans with your neighbors – you can save yourself a great deal of time by putting their minds at ease right at the start

2 Glass roofs add a dynamic quality to additions. In temperate climates it is best to choose low-E glass, which is highly insulating and so helps prevent heat loss.
3 A glassed-in box at the rear of a townhouse allows the yard to be enjoyed in all weather.

Building work

Constructing an addition is similar to building a house from scratch, albeit on a smaller scale. The same broad stages have to take place: site preparation, the laying of foundations, ground-floor construction, erection of the shell, roofing, and so on. See pages 94–5 for the sequence of work.

There are, however, certain differences. Chief among these is that the new addition will have to be connected in some way to the existing property. In the case of ground-floor additions at the side or rear, this generally entails creating an opening in an exterior wall – and may, in fact, mean an entire wall is taken down to fully absorb the new space. To compensate for the loss of this load-bearing element, a beam or RSJ (rolled-steel joist) will have to be installed over the new opening. The same applies for additions built over existing additions, unless there is a convenient window that can be lengthened to provide access. Roof additions similarly require access via a staircase to lower levels.

Roof and upper-level additions will significantly increase the load on foundations. You will need expert advice as to whether the foundations can bear this additional weight. The foundations of rear and side additions will have to be tied into existing foundations, and service connections made in all cases.

1 Extending sideways can provide enough room to reconfigure internal areas without losing too much garden space. Here, folding glass doors completely open up the end wall of the house, merging indoors with out.
2 A glass rooftop extension sends light down into lower levels and forms the access point to a roof deck.
3 The ultimate in minimalism – a glass box with glass beams – serves as a contemporary garden room.

Style and character

When you are planning to extend your home, you should spend some time (along with your architect or designer) thinking about architectural character. The planning department will also have a say in the appearance of your addition, especially if it is visible from the street or the main frontage of your home.

In general, there are two routes to a successful result. The first is to extend your home using the same materials and detailing as the existing property, so that what is new blends imperceptibly with what was already there. If your home is in an historic area, you may be required to follow this approach in any case. An alternative strategy is to opt for a bold contrast, in terms of both the materials used and the architectural style adopted – a lightweight, contemporary glass and steel box, for example, can be a highly effective addition to a Victorian or Edwardian property, with both old and new styles being robust enough to hold their own. What never seems to work are those near misses, stylistically speaking, where the addition represents a half-hearted attempt to replicate the original detailing, but does not quite manage to disguise its newness.

If you are planning an addition at the back of your house, bear in mind that the builders, their equipment and materials may have to come through your house to reach the site if there is no other means of access, which, in back-to-back townhouses, there usually is not.

Sheds & Outbuildings

It was always clear that the increasing trend for people to work from home, all or part of the time, was going to have an impact on the way we use our domestic space. However, perhaps the most surprising change that this demographic shift has brought in its wake has been the reinvention of the shed.

Sheds have long had a special appeal – entire books have been devoted to their peculiar charm and quirky uses – and there is good reason for this. On the face of it, the garden shed's raison d'être might be to serve as the repository for the lawnmower, tools and plant pots. In practice, these unpretentious outbuildings have more often become the ruminant haunts of those (chiefly men) eager to spend tranquil hours away from the household, either doing nothing much or pursuing a hobby.

Nowadays, in many back yards, the shed has been smartened up and annexed as a useful working space. The companies that specialize in producing these up-market versions report that women working from home are their best customers.

1 Few tree houses are as elegantly crafted as this wood-clad cabin on an aerial platform slung between trees. Even if you are constructing a more ad hoc example for your kids to play in, always consult the local planning department – it is not unknown for tree houses to fall foul of planning law.

The chief allure of the shed is its separateness – once you are ensconced in the shed, it is easy to divorce yourself from everyday household demands

Working retreats

Many writers, such as Roald Dahl, Philip Pullman and Margaret Drabble, have long valued the shed as a haven, where the concentrated work of the imagination could be done in peace and quiet, away from the demands of domestic life and the incessant ringing of the telephone. Other professionals are increasingly finding that the shed provides the necessary psychological – and physical – separation from domestic life that makes for productive working conditions. My son Tom runs a number of food-related businesses from a shed in his back yard that originally served as a studio for a rock musician and subsequently enjoyed a brief period as a bar with beer on tap before its present incarnation as a work space.

The chief allure of the shed is, of course, its separateness. The journey to work may consist only of a few paces down the garden path, rather than a long commute, but it is a journey nonetheless. Once you are ensconced in the shed, it is easy to divorce yourself from everyday household demands. At the same time, while you remain at one remove, you are close enough to be on hand should the need arise – to take deliveries, for example, or to let in the plumber. And, of course, cellphone and wireless Internet connections mean you can still easily be in touch with the world outside – should you wish to be.

1 The shed as writer's retreat is nothing new. This shed at Ayot St. Lawrence in Hertfordshire is where George Bernard Shaw wrote his plays. It is set on a turntable so that it can be revolved in the direction of the sun.
2 Sheds, whether custom-made or converted, make excellent working dens away from the bustle of the rest of the household. This example features a large window in front of the desk – ideal for creative daydreaming.

1

2

Converting an existing shed

If you already own a shed, it may well be worth converting it into a work space to ease pressure on the rest of your home. The feasibility of such a project, however, depends on the size and condition of the existing shed and on whether you can afford to lose the storage space that the shed is presently providing. If you are a gardener, for example, and there is nowhere else to keep tools, converting a shed into a work space will simply shift your storage problems elsewhere.

A strong shed of a decent size can be simply equipped with the addition of insulation, upgraded surfaces and finishes, shelving and office furniture. At the very least you will need to run an electrical supply out to the shed; you may need a telephone line, too (or not, if seclusion is what you are after). Always enlist the services of a qualified electrician to carry out such work: cables have to be buried at a depth where they will not be disturbed by animals. Another essential is to make sure the shed is absolutely secure – perhaps even has an alarm – especially if you will be wanting to leave equipment in it overnight, as you are less likely to hear burglars breaking into a shed at the back of your yard than attempting to force your front door.

Prefab solutions

If you do not already own a shed, or if it would not provide adequate conditions, even with a refit, for the type of work you will be undertaking, you may wish to invest in a prefab, or ready-made, shed from one of a growing number of companies that are currently producing designs for the domestic market. Many of these sheds are available with all electrical connections and insulation already installed. Some can be lifted into place by a crane if access poses a problem, as it does in many streets of townhouses where yards are tucked away behind the houses.

3

3

More of an upmarket cabin than a shed, these self-contained home offices are generally wood-framed and-clad. Some resemble beach huts; others are more akin to chalets. Many companies offer a customization service, so you can specify particular interior fixtures, such as built-in shelving, storage and work surfaces.

Planning permits

Small sheds do not, of course, require planning permission. The vagaries of the planning system being what they are, however, it is generally advisable to consult your local planning department if you are intending to install a prefab home office at the back of your yard. There may be restrictions with respect to siting or size. Better to be safe than sorry.

3 The Garden House, a weekend retreat on the outskirts of Rotterdam, is a structure in three parts, with only one section (the kitchen) attached to a concrete foundation. The other two sections are on wheels and attach to a number of different points using clips and tension straps. Twelve different configurations of the space are possible.

Sheds & Outbuildings

Converted outbuildings

While sheds may be snug and intimate, they are never going to provide the floor area or facilities you need if you are running a business from home that employs others or requires substantial workshop or storage space. If you are fortunate enough to own property with redundant outbuildings sited on it – stables, barns, and the like – such structures may be ideal for your purpose. My old agricultural buildings in the country have been converted into a small woodworking factory with the blessing of the local planning department. Even if you do not require larger premises at the moment, fledgling businesses do grow – at least, hopefully – and you may welcome the additional space before long.

Planning is often an issue here. Some planning departments welcome change of use from, say, agricultural to commercial, as it is employment-generating. Others are more reluctant, particularly if neighbors might object to increased traffic or activity next door. Whichever is the case in your area, your local planning department should be your first call. You will not be able to proceed without permission.

The actual process of conversion and the building work required depends, naturally, on the type of structure, its condition and the use you intend for it. If the outbuilding is dilapidated, one option would be to demolish it and construct premises to your own specification – which may be cheaper in the long run than a program of conversion and renovation. Such a scheme would probably require permission.

1

Stand-alone structures
Many of the stand-alone structures occupying yards in city and country alike are neither sheds nor outbuildings. Rather, they could be described as additions that are not connected to the main property in any way, but serve as annexes to the general living space. One London family, finding themselves increasingly short of space, hired an architect for just such a building. The award-winning result, a sinuous single-story structure, provides the main living area, with the house now entirely given over to service functions – sleeping, bathing, cooking and eating areas. The structure itself is mirrored along one side to reflect the garden planting and dematerialize its bulk. The process of designing and constructing such an outbuilding is not dissimilar to that of creating an addition, except that there is no need for the

The process of designing and constructing an outbuilding is not dissimilar to that of creating an addition, except that there is no need for the two buildings to be linked in any structural way

two buildings to be linked in any structural way. A covered walkway linking the two can be a good idea as a protection in bad weather; however, as the distance between the main house and the secondary building will not be great, this is not essential.

1 This award-winning pavilion was designed to accommodate a family's passion for table tennis. The undulating structure responds to its immediate site, while the mirror cladding reflects plantings. Inside is space for other hobbies, as well as room to put up overnight guests.
2 A number of companies now offer sheds and outbuildings, specifically designed for use as home offices. Wooden framing and cladding is typical.
3 A shed interior neatly outfitted with shelving and closed storage. If the shed will house expensive equipment, make sure there is adequate security.

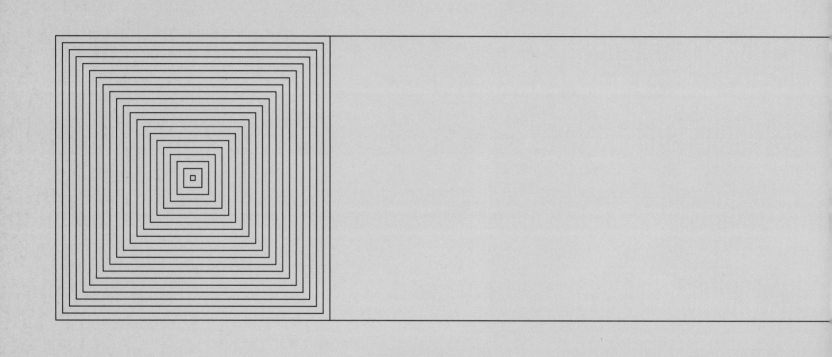

PART 2
SMALL SPACE SPECIFICS
AREA BY AREA

Multipurpose Spaces & Studios

The ultimate challenge in small-space living is the single multipurpose space or studio. Of course, much depends on the size of the space in question – a loft, after all, may be a multipurpose space and be generously scaled. It is generally accepted, however, that "studio," as in "studio apartment," implies a more circumscribed area and a Bohemian style of life – what used to be called a bachelor or bedsit, with its rather dreary connotations of privation and temporary residence.

As previously discussed in the section on open-concept layouts (see pages 40–1), there are both advantages and disadvantages to the type of arrangement where a single area serves more than one function. Lack of privacy and amplified sound are some of the drawbacks; an easy flow of activity and an inclusive spirit, perhaps, the principal advantages. It cannot be denied, however, that compact multipurpose spaces demand exceptionally tight planning and careful thought – as well as a degree of sacrifice.

1 One-space living demands careful planning. The layout of this studio apartment is defined by the central staircase leading to the sleeping platform, which separates the main living/dining area from a home office on the lower level, without compromising light or views.

Basic strategies

Living in multipurpose areas requires a somewhat different mindset from living in homes that are more conventionally laid out, where separate rooms are assigned to specific functions. A period of thorough assessment is crucial to help you identify what you really need and want, and what is optional or surplus to requirements.

Ease the demands on the space as far as possible by conducting a serious review of your possessions. All homes, however small, require storage space, but storage cannot be the prime function of a multipurpose area, or no other activity will be well served. Pare down your belongings to what is strictly necessary, even if it means doing without an entire category of possessions altogether.

Think about areas of activity, rather than "rooms." Some activities – eating and cooking, for example – are naturally easy to bracket together. A private area where you sleep can also serve in the daytime as a quiet place to work or study.

In terms of both spatial design and decorating, the trick is to unify the space as much as possible while making clear the distinction between different areas of activity. This can be a delicate balance to achieve. One approach is to keep backgrounds plain and neutral and to signal shifts of function with lighting, screens and semi-partitions (half-height, half-width or both). Try to keep sightlines uncluttered so the space can still be seen as a whole.

Opt for furniture and fixtures that are discreet and multipurpose, rather than traditional designs that shout out their function. A divan bed lends itself to being used as an additional seating area in the daytime, for example, while a bed with an obvious frame or headboard does not. Modular seating is more self-effacing than conventional sofas and armchairs.

Multipurpose Spaces & Studios

Designing the layout

In multipurpose spaces, especially small ones, every square inch of floor space will count. Spend some time working it out on paper first and trying out different options to see which delivers the greatest degree of practicality and makes the best use of space. Because precision is so important, scale drawings are essential; templates of furniture and fixtures, which you can move around on the drawings, are also useful. See page 23 for how to measure your space and draw it on paper. Alternatively, you might hire an architect or interior designer to come up with a plan. The best solutions for multipurpose areas often rely heavily on built-in features, which may need to be custom-designed and built.

1 This minimal apartment in Barcelona reduces the necessities of life down to what can be contained in two big boxes. Inspired by steamer trunks, with their fitted compartments, the basic idea is that the boxes are closed when the apartment is not occupied, preventing dust and unnecessary objects from accumulating. The "bed box" contains a double bed, clothes closets (the doors of which serve to screen dressing and undressing), a shelf for suitcases, a mirror, two night tables with lamps, a drawer for pillows and blankets and a sliding tray for any small possessions. The "kitchen box" is similarly articulated, with pull-out tables and shelves.

2 A simple idea for one-space living is to contain the bed within a screened enclosure – like a contemporary version of a four-poster with its curtains.

3 Grouping services into a central core makes good sense in multipurpose layouts. Here, a kitchen area is screened behind a high concrete counter and a work area is just visible beyond.

■ **Natural light** Think about which activity would benefit most from natural light and try to arrange the layout accordingly. If you work from home during the day, setting up a desk or study area near a window will aid your concentration. If you cook only in the evening – or do not cook much at all – you can rely chiefly on artificial light to illuminate a kitchen area.

■ **Intimacy** Most of us sleep easier in surroundings that provide some degree of enclosure. Think about screening a sleeping area in some way, even if privacy is not an issue.

■ **Services** The existing service arrangements – especially water and drainage – may well dictate where you can site a kitchen within a multipurpose space. If this means the layout is less than ideal – and you have enough money in your budget – you can consult an architect, plumber or engineer to see whether it would be feasible to make alterations to existing arrangements.

■ **Power outlets** Increasing the number of power outlets in an area is generally less disruptive and expensive than altering other types of services. You will probably need more outlets than you think – the last thing you want is a spaghetti of wiring trailing all over the floor. The more power outlets there are, the more flexible the space will be.

■ **Recesses and alcoves** Make use of any irregularity to build in storage or other installed elements.

■ **Ventilation** If your multipurpose space includes a kitchen and eating area, you will need an efficient exhaust fan to ventilate cooking odors.

■ **Concealment** Try to conceal the functional or working parts of the space as much as possible. Compact kitchens or home offices that fold away behind cabinet doors minimize visual distraction when you are using the space to relax or entertain.

■ **Articulation** Fold-down, pull-out or hinged furniture and fixtures can help you make the most of space without compromising basic practicality.

Multipurpose Spaces & Studios

Lofts

Options for workable layouts dramatically increase if there is enough ceiling height in the space to accommodate a loft level comfortably. The ideal is, of course, a "double-height space," which means you can increase usable floor area to a significant degree. Reasonably high ceilings – less than double-height but greater than average – also permit sleeping areas to be shifted up on to a platform, provided you do not feel cramped and claustrophobic lying under a low ceiling.

1 Older properties often have very high ceilings, which means you can insert a loft or platform in part of the space and significantly increase usable floor area. An open flight of stairs may not be ideal for anyone suffering from vertigo.

2 An unusual treatment for a loft, this strong netting in the form of an overscaled hammock provides a place for lounging around.

3 You do not need full head room if you are going to use a loft simply as a sleeping platform. A skylight overcomes any sense of claustrophobia.

Service cores

If you have enough room at your disposal, one way to arrange a multipurpose space is to group services in a single core, either stacked vertically or grouped centrally. This type of arrangement often makes a more dynamic use of space than layouts that essentially hug the perimeter of the area. A central service core can be hidden from the main space by a circular partition or by half-height dividers. Alternatively, it can be fully enclosed within a box or pod-like structure.

2

3

■ Adding a loft is structural work because you are increasing the load on existing walls. You will need an architect to design the structure of the new level and its means of support. Platforms can be constructed in the same way; simpler, however, is to make use of the top of a freestanding structure.

■ Depending on how much space you have, stairs or other means of access can make a dramatic focal point or be more reticent and space-saving. See pages 46–7 for space-saving stairs.

■ Siting is critical. It is usually best to add a loft or platform on a blank wall where it will not interrupt views or block natural light from existing windows.

■ Think about how best to use the area under the loft or platform. Kitchens, bathrooms, service areas and built-in storage can be slotted into the space, leaving the main floor area clear.

■ Size is another important issue. A narrow loft or gallery will probably only permit a single use – sleeping or working, for example. Too generous a loft will overwhelm the level below and block light and views. In the case of platforms, where use is restricted by head height, you need only allow enough space for a bed, with a margin around the perimeter for access and changing bed linen.

■ Decide whether you want the loft to remain open or whether it should be screened in some way. Transparent glass screens provide some degree of separation and security. Other options include metal mesh panels, or even lift-up panels hoisted by rope and pulley. Platforms are often left fully open, without even a guardrail – not an option, however, if you are someone who tosses and turns in their sleep and might roll out of bed.

Living Areas

1 Living areas do not need to be vast to provide room for relaxation, but they should be as uncluttered as possible, so that you are not constantly reminded of pressing chores that remain to be done or other household matters. Enclosed spaces, such as alcoves, window seats or this rounded nook, are always very appealing places of refuge – somewhere, literally, to curl up with a book.

These days, no area in the home is as difficult to define as the living room. We all know the principal purposes of bedrooms, bathrooms and home offices. "Living" areas, however, remain rather more amorphous, especially as much of daily life increasingly seems to happen in the kitchen. This lack of a settled definition or function can be all too evident – either the space is given over to a multitude of different activities that cannot be accommodated elsewhere and that sometimes war with each other or it remains largely unused for much of the time. Many living areas that are decorated and furnished to impress the neighbors fall into the latter category.

1

Given the busy, stressful lives that most of us lead, it seems perfectly clear what role a living area should play, and that is to provide a place to relax and enjoy the company of family and friends, listen to music or watch TV. For that reason, comfort should be what your living area offers first and foremost.

By comfort I do not merely mean well-constructed and upholstered sofas and chairs, though furniture of a decent quality is important, I also mean lack of visual clutter, sensitive lighting and unobtrusive media equipment: a sense that there is space to breathe, if you like. Of course, when your home is on the small side, this is more difficult to achieve; but, then again, you will need it all the more.

■ Think about the activities that your living area currently serves. Are there any that could be shifted elsewhere to free up space and create a calmer atmosphere? Many activities bring with them requirements for storage – and clutter can impinge on a mood of relaxation.

■ Enlarging existing openings or improving a living area's connection with the yard, deck or balcony can help open up the space. See page 37.

■ When choosing seat furniture, make sure it supports the body, particularly the lower back. A comfortable room is naturally hospitable: a room that is decorated and furnished to spell out the message "look but don't touch" is edgy and offputting. I always say that you know you have got it right when guests or visitors feel free to sit down and take off their jackets (or slip off their shoes) without being asked.

■ Pay particular attention to lighting. Highlight areas of display, bounce light off the walls and ceiling and use shaded table lamps to create intimate focal points. See pages 66–77.

■ Mirrors may be a clichéd solution for enhancing a sense of space, but that is because they work. Large expanses of mirror above a fireplace, or mirrors placed where they reflect a window or door, multiply views.

■ Get the little things right. Details matter in a small space, particularly one that is on public view. Choose good-quality door handles and switches plates.

Home media solutions

If pressed, I suppose most people would define their living room as the place where they watch TV, though that definition, in today's multiscreen households, does not universally hold. Nevertheless, most living rooms do operate as home media centers of some sort, even if you are watching the wildlife documentary by yourself while your children are glued to a reality show upstairs.

While people have become a little less coy about admitting how much of their leisure time is devoted to watching the box, there is still no need for media equipment to dominate the living area. Unfortunately, the smaller the area in question, the greater the risk that this will happen. And it is not simply the TV that can assume too much importance, but all the rest of the electronic gadgetry that keeps us amused – CD players, speakers, computers, VCRs and DVD players as well.

One of the problems with home media systems is the rapid pace of technology. Some of us still treasure our vinyl and hang on to turntables to play it on, despite the fact that current technology now allows us to store our entire music collection on a device that will fit easily into a pocket. Similarly, instead of rebuying on DVD all the films we have enjoyed on video, many of us maintain several different systems at once, knowing that the next technological generation cannot be too far in the future, which means giving room to a VCR as well as a DVD player, and so on. There is no ready solution

The problem with home media systems is the pace of technology – some of us still treasure our vinyl, despite the fact that we can store our music collection in a pocket

for this – at least no inexpensive one – but you may wish to keep the more up-to-date equipment in your living area and relegate the older systems to other parts of the home, where they will not compromise the sense of space and overall atmosphere to such a degree.

If you are able to upgrade your media equipment, take advantage of the fact that powerful sound (and processing in the case of computers) now comes in very small packages. And while no one would call flat-screen TVs small or discreet, they are very thin, which makes them easier to conceal behind sliding panels. For the ultimate in discretion, integral music systems with centralized controls allow you to pipe sound to different areas through concealed speakers.

1

2

Tidy wires

Rapid advances in wireless technology, or Wi-Fi, may mean that we will very soon see the end of a mass of cables snaking across the floors of our homes. In the meantime, make sure you have enough power outlets, so that you avoid overloading sockets or being treated to the ugly sight of a jumble of tangled cords and cables. Sleeves that tidy cables into a single package can also be a good idea.

3

1 If you have an extensive collection of CDs and DVDs, try to store them neatly and accessibly. In a small space, wall-hung racks or special CD/DVD towers make too much of a feature of such items and, if your collection is constantly expanding, will be quickly outgrown. This arrangement, where CDs are stored under the low shelf on which media equipment is kept, is a good solution.
2 An alternative solution is to keep your music or film collection concealed in built-in storage, as here. You might wish to separate favorites from your archive so you don't waste a great deal of time hunting for what you want. Serious collectors might consider arranging discs alphabetically or by theme.
3 With the advent of flat-screen TVs, sets are much less dominant than they used to be and stow away more readily behind panels of built-in storage. Place the TV set on a shelf at a convenient viewing height.

1

Concealed storage

Small space living means that most areas in your home will have to double up as storage spaces. While open shelving can be hospitable in kitchens, for example, concealment is often a better bet in living areas, particularly for videos, CDs, DVDs, and the like, which do not offer the same aesthetic pleasure as a library of books.

■ Work with the basic layout and structure of the room and build your storage into alcoves or recesses or around doorways, as appropriate. A long horizontal row of low-level lockers can house a great many possessions and also provide space on top for seating or for display.

■ If you have sufficient room, it may be worth devoting an entire wall to built-in storage to house all manner of belongings, painting the doors or drawer fronts to match the rest of the room. Even home offices in living areas can be effectively concealed within cabinets. As with all built-in solutions, unless you are an expert at carpentry, it is essential to call in a professional to do the work.

1 A wall of sleek built-in cabinets conceals everyday possessions behind warm-toned wood doors in a living area. The TV is also hidden from view.
2 In this living area, storage for books, CDs and other accessories is hidden around the perimeter of the room behind the backs of low seating. When storage is this unobtrusive, you may well need some kind of sketch plan to remind you exactly where things are.

2

The challenge in an open-concept area is to create a sense of separation without blocking light or carving up the space

■ Containers can be used to organize a vast amount of clutter. A neat array of matching containers on open shelving provides easy access and is less expensive and disruptive than built-in solutions if you are on a tight budget.

Dividers and partitions

Living areas that are given over to several different functions – perhaps relaxing and eating, or relaxing and working – can seem very disjointed without an element of separation between the different areas of activity. The challenge is to achieve this without blocking light or carving up the space unnecessarily. Open freestanding room dividers are often a good option, as they combine storage with display and permit future alterations to room layout. Standing folding screens can also be used to shield a desk from the rest of the living space. Alternatively, you can simply arrange furniture in such a way as to make the distinction clear – a sofa, for example, positioned across the room, rather than against the wall, effectively divides the area in two.

Surfaces and finishes

Nothing imparts a sense of character and quality better than natural materials. This is not about furnishing your living area as a showcase but about taking a long-term view and choosing surfaces and finishes that will stand the test of time and improve as they age and wear. The great advantage of small space living is that you can afford better-quality materials when you don't need to cover or finish a large area. A hardwood, rather than laminate, floor, for example, gives the entire space a feeling of integrity and generosity.

3

4

3 A frosted glass panel above a low solid partition separates the living area from the rest of a multipurpose space. Transparent partitions make the separation of activities clear without blocking light.
4 Living areas are often called upon to serve more than one function when space is very tight. Here, a home office is completely enclosed by sliding screens, so that it can be masked from the rest of the space when not in use.

Kitchens & Eating Areas

Over the past few decades, the trend for the kitchen to serve essentially as an informal living area has been one of the more significant shifts in the way we live. As a result, the large, inclusive kitchen, where family and friends can gather and where socializing is of equal importance to food preparation, has become a priority for many people, even those who are not particularly keen on cooking. Small kitchens, which used to be the norm in the average household, have never been less appealing – it is as if their spatial limitations signify a certain meanness of spirit, or a poor appetite for life. However, if you are very short on space, you will have to accept that your kitchen will probably be more circumscribed than the generous ideal exemplified by the kitchen as the "hub of the home."

There are two ways of ameliorating this shortfall. One is to incorporate a compact kitchen area within a multipurpose living space, a strategy that achieves the sense of inclusion that we value so highly these days. The other is to design a separate small room as a well-organized one-person kitchen and gain pleasure from the efficiency of the work space.

1

1 A narrow kitchen with angled wall and ceiling planes has been simply outfitted for maximum efficiency. Small kitchens, provided they are not overburdened with too much equipment, can be surprisingly workable.

Keep it simple

Many professional cooks (and many keen amateurs, too) actively prefer small kitchens because they offer ease of operation and a high degree of control, with everything you need within easy reach. (Of course, if you do not entertain very often and eat out more often than in, a small kitchen where you can fend for yourself in a basic way makes perfect sense – there is nothing worse than a large "trophy" kitchen that no one ever cooks in and is often installed at vast expense to impress the neighbors.)

Whichever approach you choose, the actual working area of the kitchen will inevitably be limited to a certain degree – which not only means less counter space, but less storage space, too. For this reason, you will have to be particularly ruthless about what you keep in the kitchen – everything from small appliances to foodstuffs and basic provisions will need to earn its keep.

Keen cooks tend to be keen on kitchen equipment, too, and often accumulate specialized utensils and gadgets. Seasoned cooks, however, can produce exceptional results using only the most basic equipment – a set of good knives, a couple of good saucepans, a frying pan, a casserole dish and the like. Review your batterie de cuisine and try to reduce pressure on storage and counter space by discarding what you rarely use.

All-purpose cookware, tableware and glassware prevents duplication and makes storage easier, since items will be uniformly shaped and sized – glasses you can use for water, wine or juice can be readily stacked, for example.

Similarly, do make sure your shopping list, and supermarket purchases, keep in step with what you actually cook and consume. Your pantry essentials may well differ from mine, but the most important thing is that they reflect your tastes accurately and consistently.

1 This variation on the galley kitchen features a wall of storage with inset cooktop and a facing half-height cabinet that allows views through to the rest of the space.

Designing the layout

Most successful small kitchens are built-in, since built-in solutions exploit available space to a greater degree than freestanding or modular designs, which usually require more floor area. Built-in kitchens also present fewer obstacles that might get in the way when you are moving from fridge to oven, for example. At the same time, they look neater and more seamless, which makes them easier to work in.

The work triangle

For many years, kitchen planning has been based around the concept of the "work triangle," which specifies optimum distances between the three main areas of kitchen activity (sink, fridge and cooktop/oven). Ideally, the total distance (the sum of the sides of the triangle) should be no greater than 20 ft. (6 m), with each working area at least 36 in. (90 cm) apart. In a small kitchen there will be little risk that the main areas of activity will be overly remote; instead, you will have to ensure you have enough elbow room. The most critical area is between the sink and the cooktop, where most food preparation takes place. This is where the longest stretch of worktop should be.

Points to consider

■ Sinks and cooktops should be positioned at least 16 in. (40 cm) from the corner for ease of use.
■ Group tall cabinets at each end of the worktop to keep the main preparation area clear.
■ Work with existing services as far as possible – it is expensive and disruptive to change. Plan your layout starting with the current position of the sink. Dishwashers should be sited near the sink for ease of plumbing.
■ Make sure you take into account how much space you will need to open dishwasher and oven doors.
■ Whether self-contained or integrated in a living area, kitchens must have efficient ventilation and extraction.

1

Types of layout

Most of the common types of kitchen layouts are suitable for small areas, with the exception of the island kitchen, which does demand more generous floor area. It is the shape of the space at your disposal, as much as the size, that will determine which solution works best for you.

■ The single-line layout is best for long narrow kitchens or a kitchen area arranged along the length of one wall. Ideally, you need at least 10 ft. (3 m) of wall space. Sliding cabinet doors are more space-saving than hinged ones. If the kitchen is part of a multipurpose space, you can screen the entire kitchen area with sliding or folding doors.

■ The galley kitchen, where cabinets and counters are fitted along facing walls, is another efficient compact layout. You need a minimum of 4 ft. (1.2 m) between the facing cabinets.

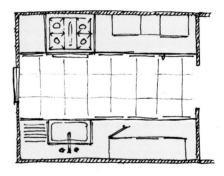

■ An L-shaped layout, where cabinets are arranged along two adjacent walls (or along one wall and under a peninsula projecting into the room at right angles) is a good way of integrating a kitchen into a general living space.

■ U-shaped layouts can also be successful where space is restricted, provided there is enough room for the arms of the U to be at least 6½ ft. (2 m) apart.

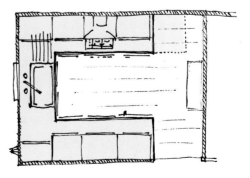

1

2

3

1 A compact kitchen can be shut away behind doors. The counter/worktop doubles up as a breakfast bar.
2 Plan kitchen storage carefully to make the most of space and keep unlovely equipment out of view. Fold-down ironing boards that fit neatly into cabinets are space-saving.

Space-saving and space-enhancing ideas

There are a variety of ways in which you can save space if your kitchen is cramped. Equally important is to enhance whatever space you have through well-considered decorating and design choices. Small kitchens can be remarkably comfortable to use if you get the fit right and pay attention to details.

Points to consider

■ Pull-out or fold-down features make the most of limited space. If you are short of counter space, for example, a pull-out worktop can significantly improve your working efficiency. A fold-down tabletop makes it possible to eat in a small kitchen. Other similarly articulated features include fold-down ironing boards that are stored within utility cabinets.

■ Slimline and small-scale appliances can be a good bet, provided they are able to serve your needs. If you prefer to shop weekly, for example, and what you buy generally fills a fridge of standard size, do not expect a mini fridge to add to your efficiency or quality of life, no matter how much floor area it saves.

■ Customize the interiors of kitchen cabinets with drawer dividers, racks, containers and other accessories that allow you to fully use available storage space. Lazy Susans that fit into corners permit you to exploit what would otherwise be dead space.

■ Cabinets that are raised up on feet, or ones where the plinth is omitted, look visually lighter than those that are flush with the floor.

■ Keep surfaces and finishes plain and muted. White or neutral tones and reflective materials such as glass, tile and stainless steel are naturally space-enhancing.

■ Pay particular attention to lighting, both natural and artificial. You can improve the quality of light in an enclosed or internal area – and improve views and vistas – by installing interior windows or portholes. Similarly, you can make a self-contained kitchen more integrated with the rest of your home and make the connection between the two more efficient by removing the door and the portion of wall above it. Recessed or fitted types of light, such as downlights, make sense in a small, built-in space. These should be carefully positioned so that there is no risk that you will be working in your own shadow.

3 A small L-shaped kitchen still provides enough space for a compact eating area. The table hinges down from the wall, while the stools slot neatly together when not in use.

Kitchen cabinet

Responding to the need for compact kitchen designs, some manufacturers (such as Boffi, below) are now producing kitchens that are integrated within a single freestanding cabinet for maximum space-saving. These designs, which may incorporate a sink, oven, cooktop and fridge, along with storage, only require service connections to be made fully functional.

Kitchens & Eating Areas

Meals shared with family and friends remain important social occasions and add immeasurably to the enjoyment of life

1 Formal dining in a separate room is more or less ruled out if you are living in a small space, but that does not mean you have to forgo the pleasures of shared mealtimes. A table placed at right angles to the kitchen in this open-concept space means it is easier to ignore kitchen activity during meals.

2 The eating area in this tiny kitchen is defined by a wall painted blue and a narrow counter just wide enough for a place setting.

Eating areas

Cooking and eating are activities that are naturally so closely related that it is hardly surprising that the formal dining room has become virtually extinct. With informality a defining characteristic of today's lifestyles and pressure on space ever increasing, the notion of maintaining a separate room for what is at best limited use can seem misguided, to say the least.

Nevertheless, eating is not simply refueling. Meals shared with family and friends remain important social occasions and add immeasurably to the enjoyment of life. Even when space is limited, you need to provide a place where people can sit down together, even if that area serves other functions the rest of the time.

4

3 In a space where the kitchen is visible from the eating area, it is best to screen appliances and preparation areas from view as far as possible. It is also a good idea to put lighting on dimmer controls, so that you can vary the focus of attention. The long unit that separates the kitchen from

the dining table features storage on both sides.
4 A U-shaped kitchen layout incorporates a deep counter that serves as a breakfast bar.

■ Fold-down or pull-out tabletops within the kitchen area. Few such arrangements provide enough table space to accommodate more than a couple of place settings, but they are useful for breakfasts, lunches or light suppers.

■ Peninsulas or half-height room dividers that screen a kitchen area from the living space can be used as breakfast bars on the "living side," with cabinets and appliances facing into the kitchen area.

■ Tables that extend, or into which additional leaves can be inserted, are good solutions for the occasions when you entertain larger numbers.

■ Where the kitchen occupies a small self-contained area, you will need to create a dining area within the living space. Site it out of the main traffic routes and plan the furniture layout to make a clear distinction between the different activities, perhaps by using room dividers. Otherwise, exploit the shape of the space. An L-shaped room, for example, allows you to position a dining area in the shorter arm of the L.

■ When your eating area is part of a multipurpose space, it can also do double duty as a work area between mealtimes. The transition between one activity and the other will seem more natural if you choose a table and chairs that are simple and generic in design and that do not look as though they are intended to be used solely for dining.

■ Light the table with a hanging lamp positioned low enough to avoid glare and high enough not to obscure views across the table. Some hanging lamps can be attached to the wall and swung across when required.

■ Control kitchen lighting with dimmer switches so the working nature of the space is less emphasized when you are eating in the same area.

■ Do not neglect the potential of outdoor areas – eating outside can be a real pleasure. Improving the connection between kitchen and yard, roof deck or balcony means you will be more likely to take advantage of good weather when it comes.

Bedrooms

Sleeping is one activity that is not always adversely affected by spatial limitations. As long as your bed is big enough and there is sufficient space around the perimeter for access and changing bed linen, you can rest as easily and comfortably in a small bedroom as you can in a larger one. Smaller bedrooms are often cosier and more intimate than vast master bedrooms in any case, which enhances their role as tranquil retreats from the rest of the household.

All creatures seek out enclosed spaces to sleep in, where they will feel less vulnerable and exposed. We have similar instincts, which is why small bedrooms can be surprisingly appealing. We do not, however, spend all our time in the bedroom in a state of blissful unconsciousness. Other functions also intrude, notably dressing and undressing, and storing clothes, shoes, accessories and makeup. The demand for storage is what puts the squeeze on bedroom space. When your bedroom is small, you have two main options. The first is to keep your clothing elsewhere; the second is to accommodate it within the bedroom without compromising the space's essential role as a private refuge.

1 Mirrors help make the most of natural light in a bedroom. Even a small bedroom can be a tranquil retreat, especially if you are able to keep your clothes closet elsewhere, such as on a landing or in a hallway.

As the bedroom is necessarily dominated by a large piece of furniture, the less you subsequently put into it, the better. While most of the time we spend in the bedroom we spend asleep, oblivious to our surroundings, those moments before sleep overtakes us and after we wake up in the morning are critical times of the day. It is far better to wind down or to face a new day in a calm, serene space than to wake up or drift off amid a sea of clutter.

Strategies to consider

■ Avoid central overhead lighting at all costs. Glare is always a risk with central lighting; that risk is multiplied when you are lying down. Atmospheric alternatives include sidelighting, uplighting and shaded bedside table lamps. Dimmer controls are invaluable in bedrooms.

■ Soft materials create a warm and inviting mood. Carpet and natural-fiber floor coverings are kind to bare feet and insulate against sound. Curtains and fabric blinds filter the light in a gentle, diffused way. Good-quality bed linen – crisp cotton or linen sheets and duvet covers, woolen blankets and throws, and plump pillows provide comfort next to the skin.

■ If you are easily disturbed by the light, line curtains or blinds with blackout material.

■ Choose wall colors according to the orientation of the space. Whites and blues can be too chilly in rooms that face north or east. Creams and warm neutrals are a better bet (see pages 56–9).

■ Try to plan your space so that the bathroom is en suite to your bedroom.

Bedrooms

Sleeping platforms

Creating a platform to serve as a sleeping area can help you make the most of the space at your disposal, whether you are dealing with a single multipurpose space or a small bedroom. Conventional beds tend to provide useful storage space underneath, where you can keep bed linen, shoes, sweaters and similar bulky items in drawers or containers; some beds have built-in drawer space. With high-level beds, the opportunity to use the space beneath as a storage area is greatly increased, with the advantage that the sleeping area is kept free from extraneous clutter.

Raised sleeping areas can vary from simple platforms – the top of a built-in storage unit, for example – to lofts accessed by stairs. Head room is a critical factor: such arrangements do not require a double-height space, but ceiling height has to be greater than average, at least enough to allow you to sit up in bed without banging your head. Make sure the platform or raised level can be accessed safely; if you are nimble enough to hop up and down a ladder, it should be securely anchored.

If you live alone, or if the sleeping platform is in a self-contained area, there is no need to worry about further enclosure (see pages 130–1). In any case, views across the space can help counteract any feeling of claustrophobia. Otherwise, you may wish to screen the platform or loft in some way. A guardrail or some form of protective barrier is also a good idea.

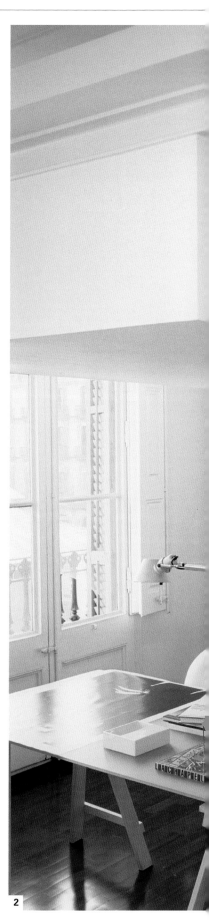

1 A simple sleeping platform is raised up over built-in storage cabinetry faced in tongue-and-groove paneling.
2 A low sleeping platform-cum-loft is suspended under the ceiling and accessed via open stepped storage. The total absence of handrails or guardrails means this type of arrangement is best suited to the sure-footed – as well as those who are sound sleepers.
3 A low bed positioned under an open staircase makes the most of space where there is not full head room.

With high-level beds, the opportunity to use the space beneath as a storage area is greatly increased

3

Low-level beds

One of the simplest ways of enhancing the sense of space in a small sleeping area is to opt for a low-level bed or sleep on a (well-sprung) mattress on the floor. Beds, like sofas, are large and dominant; raised bed frames and headboards only make them more conspicuous. Low-level beds are a good solution for sleeping platforms and areas such as converted attics, where head height may be less than average.

Sleeping pods

Another way of providing a quiet enclave within an open-plan space is to site the bed in a box, pod or capsule – any form of enclosure that provides the privacy you require. The idea is similar to the service core, which is a standard feature of many loft layouts. Depending on the degree of separation that you require, the pod can be fully enclosed or screened with slatted blinds or translucent panels. Glass can now become opaque at the touch of a switch.

Bedrooms

Clothes storage

At the risk of repeating myself, I will say that the essential first step when it comes to tackling any storage problem is to review what you own and discard what you do not like or need. It is estimated that we wear only a fifth of the clothes we own, which effectively means that 80 percent of the area given over to clothes storage is wasted space. Get rid of the clothing that does not fit you or does not suit you, that you never wear or that has been eaten by moths, and you may well find you do not need as much storage space as you first thought.

Clothes remain in good condition for longer and are less susceptible to moth attack if they are kept in drawers, closets or wardrobes, rather than out on view, hanging from rails or piled on open shelves. When you are living in a small space, this means built-in storage. Traditional storage furniture is both visually intrusive and less spatially efficient.

Options for built-in clothes storage include mass-market versions, available in a variety of styles and materials, specialized closet systems, which may be customized to your own requirements, and custom-made closet organizers, designed and built to your own specifications. Whichever route you choose, it is best to devote an entire wall to built-in storage so that the final effect is more seamless and blends in with the structure of the room. Alternatively, you can use alcoves or recesses for concealed storage without losing too much usable floor area. Extend the storage from floor to ceiling so that it is seen as a continuous plane.

1 If you need to keep clothing in your bedroom, make sure it is in built-in storage concealed from view. Open clothes rails are obtrusive in small spaces and do not provide the ideal conditions for keeping clothing. These cabinets installed underneath windows provide a place for display on top.

2 Built-in storage should be as self-effacing as possible. Doors and panels can be painted to blend in with the rest of the room or made from lightweight or semi-transparent materials.

1

Clothes remain in good condition for longer and are less susceptible to moth attack if they are kept in drawers, closets or wardrobes

■ Hanging storage requires a depth of no less than 2 ft. (60 cm).

■ Drawers need a clearance of at least 3 ft. 3 in. (1 m) in front; standard hinged doors slightly more. To save space, screen shelves or hanging space with blinds or with sliding, bifold or accordion doors.

■ Make use of the back of closet doors. You can attach a full-length mirror or narrow rails for storing belts, ties and scarves.

■ Shelves at a high level are useful for storing luggage.

■ As with kitchen storage, customize the interior of drawers and cubbyholes with dividers and containers, so that you make full use of the space.

■ Translucent doors and panels, especially if they are backlit, lighten the look of built-in storage. Mirrored doors are also space-enhancing.

Dressing areas

Separate dressing rooms or dressing areas sound like an indulgence, but even when your home is small they can still represent a good use of space. Dressing areas can be quite compact and remain practical – a short vestibule, an adjacent hallway or a walk-in closet properly outfitted may be all that you require. You need to site such an area near to where you sleep or close to the bathroom for ease of access.

Children's Rooms

While small spaces do not rule out family life, it is fair to say that the arrival of children places extra demands on domestic arrangements. What was formerly compact yet workable can begin to feel quite cramped as soon as the sweet little bundle you brought home from the hospital grows into a rambunctious toddler getting into everything. When that toddler eventually gains a sibling, you may find that you need to rethink the entire way you allocate space.

At this point, many people decide to move to a larger home; if you cannot, you may find this is a good time to think about major spatial change – converting an attic, for example, or putting on an addition (see pages 96–117). In the early months you will probably want to keep your baby close to you, in a bassinet near your bed. After that, however, your child will need a room of his or her own.

Options

It makes sense, especially if you plan to increase your family, to juggle sleeping arrangements so that the biggest bedroom is the child's room. Small children need greater floor area to play and romp around, and a bedroom that provides this will ease pressure on the rest of the household. Later on, when another child comes along, a larger bedroom will be easier to share. Then, much further down the line, you may wish to switch things around again to give teenagers their own space. Teenagers, surprisingly, do not always mind having a small bedroom, provided they can customize the space as they please.

■ **Children's beds** Children's sleeping arrangements, particularly the size and type of bed, need to be reviewed at several key stages. After the first few months, when small portable bassinets are often a good solution, it is a sound idea to move the baby into a proper crib to encourage settled sleep routines. Crib that allow you to lower the mattress as the child grows provide more flexibility.

The next stage, when your child reaches the age of two or so, is the move from the crib to a proper full-sized bed. Buy the best quality you can afford and the bed may well see your child right through teenage years (though the mattress will need to be replaced at least once).

■ **Space-saving beds** Bunk beds and high-level beds that incorporate storage or play areas underneath keep floor areas as clear as possible, which is an advantage in the early years when much play is floor-based. You should not, however, allow a child under the age of five or six to sleep at the top. Guardrails are legally essential, as is a secure ladder to the upper level.

A version of the platform or high-level bed also represents a good solution for teenagers, with the space below serving as a work or study area, or simply somewhere to chill out and listen to music.

Children's Rooms

Flexible storage

Family life poses particular demands in terms of storage. Anticipation is the key to keeping on top of things and avoiding a slow but sure slide into chaos.

You cannot altogether rely on seamless concealed storage for housing children's possessions, for the simple reason that most children like to see their possessions out on view. When a child is very small, anything that you put away will be forgotten about and not used. By the time it is "rediscovered," your child may well have passed the age when he or she is interested in playing with it at all. Accept that, in the early years at least, a certain amount of visual clutter will be unavoidable. Open shelving and other forms of storage will also help you encourage your children to participate in the "game" of tidying up.

Safety

As soon as your child becomes mobile, childproof your home. Many accidents that happen in the home are preventable.
■ Place covers over all power outlets.
■ Use corner protectors if you have sharp-edged glass or metal tables or counters.

■ Make sure all tall or heavy items of storage furniture are securely anchored to the wall, to prevent them from toppling over (or being pulled over).
■ Keep trailing light cords out of children's reach – installed lighting is often a better solution than table or floor lamps in children's rooms.

■ Lock all toxic substances away, including paint, glue, bleach, garden products and prescription medicines.
■ Use safety glass for glass doors, screens or cabinetry fronts; it fractures into harmless pebbles on impact.
■ Keep an unlocked first-aid kit in an accessible location.

1

2

3

4

1 Wicker baskets make good storage containers in children's rooms. The more accessible the storage, the more chance you will have of getting your children to cooperate when it is time to tidy up.
2 Modular containers allow you to "sort and store" children's toys and belongings with ease.

If more than one child is sharing a bedroom, it can be a good idea to separate their belongings, so that each child has his or her own dedicated space to keep things.
3 A low-level shelf/countertop provides space for creative play with storage containers stowed neatly underneath.

4 Reclaimed school lockers serve as individual closets for clothing in a shared children's room. Labels indicate whose is whose.
5 Older children and teenagers often enjoy high-level sleeping platforms. The floor space underneath can double as a study area and relaxation den.

Points to consider

■ Baby equipment such as highchairs, strollers and car seats can be very bulky, though collapsible designs ease the pressure on space to some degree. Allocate a designated area where such equipment can be stored when not in use.

■ Use deep storage areas in attics, basements and the like for those clothes, toys and equipment that you are keeping to pass on to the next child.

■ Containers are invaluable for storing children's toys and belongings. Color-coding allows you to see at a glance whose is whose or to organize multipiece games and puzzles.

■ Underbed spaces make accessible storage areas. Some children's beds incorporate drawers in the base; if not, you can buy storage boxes on casters.

■ Review possessions and clothing on a regular basis. Children grow and develop quickly, and unless you discard or recycle a proportion of their belongings at each stage, you will soon find yourself overwhelmed.

■ Shelving makes good all-purpose storage – for toys, games and picture books in the early years, and books, computer games and CDs later on.

Bathrooms

1 Small, but perfectly formed. This small bathroom has been detailed with utmost precision. Glass screens and shelves make the most of available light, while the medicine cabinet and painted window frame provide accents of vibrant color.

There was a time when the average bathroom more than merited the coy tag of "the smallest room," particularly where the bathroom had been a later introduction to a period house constructed without such indoor facilities. We expect more of our bathrooms now than such cramped functionality; increasingly, the bathroom is second only to the bedroom as a place of retreat and renewal. If you have limited space at your disposal, the challenge is to satisfy such needs within a circumscribed area.

Small bathrooms have obvious drawbacks, not least of which is the difficulty of providing at least some clear space between the separate fixtures of bathtub/shower, sink and toilet. Depending on the floor area, opportunities for storage may also be somewhat curtailed. In most cases, too, you will have to forgo any notion of furnishing the bathroom with incidental pieces, such as chairs or sofas, which can add a comfortable, hospitable dimension in a more generous-sized space. All this, however, does not mean that a small bathroom cannot be a pleasant or practical place. Clever spatial planning and the right choice of fixtures will help you to make the most of what you have.

■ Which features and fixtures are absolutely essential? Which could you do without? When space is tight, you will not be able to fit in double sinks, for example.

■ Showers are more space-saving than bathtubs. But substituting a shower for a tub when you prefer soaking to showering will not add to the quality of your life – and may affect the resale value of your home. A really good, powerful shower, however, can be an acceptable alternative to a bathtub for many people.

■ Think about separating toilets from bathtubs/showers. This is often a better strategy than putting up with a cramped layout that does not provide the right psychological distance between different functions, and it should take up no more floor area.

■ Another option is to include a bathing area within the bedroom. You can separate the two spaces very simply by constructing a half-height partition behind the bed – as a type of overscaled headboard – to screen the bathing or washing area. Alternatively, you could site the tub in full view if privacy is not an issue. The more space there is around a tub, the more relaxed you will feel.

■ Treating the bathroom as a wet room – a fully waterproofed space in which the shower is not contained and drains directly to the floor – maximizes available floor area (see pages 160–1).

■ Self-contained bathroom "pods" or capsules can make good use of space within a multipurpose layout.

Bathrooms

Designing the layout

As with other tightly planned spaces, you will need to try out different layouts on paper first. Use templates of bathroom fixtures to determine the optimum arrangement. See page 23 for how to make a scale plan.

If it is not altogether clear how you are going to fit it all in, or if you find it difficult to think in three dimensions, you may wish to look into of a design service. Many large retailers, as well as specialized bathroom suppliers, provide in-store design advice, including site visits and installation packages. You will need to take along measurements of the area in question, with existing services indicated on a diagram or scale drawing. Information is usually entered into a computer program, along with your preferences in terms of color, style and type of fixture. You will then receive a 3-D representation of what the result will look like. Alternatively, for a custom-made design, you may wish to consult an architect or an interior designer, particularly if the work will involve rerouting services or obtaining permits.

1 A small bathroom in a converted attic space has been laid out so that the foot of the bathtub is positioned under the eaves, where head room is lowest. Bathroom fixtures are heavy, so if you plan to install a bathroom in a converted attic, you may need to strengthen the floor joists to a greater degree than if you were simply using the area for sleeping or working.
2 Wall-hung fixtures that keep the floor clear are naturally space-enhancing. The flooring in this bathroom extends right into the shower area.

Increasing floor area

Before you attempt to design the layout, investigate whether it is possible to win yourself more floor area. Bathrooms are often located adjacent to hallways and sometimes it is possible to move the partition wall forward by a small margin. This can make all the difference between a layout that is workable and one that is not.

Increasing wall area

To free up wall space to allow for the siting of a shower, for example, or a heated towel rail, you might consider blocking up a window. Provided there is adequate ventilation, bathrooms can be fully internal. If the bathroom has more than one window, this option can be even more attractive.

Fixtures

The right choice of bathroom fixtures can go a long way toward creating a successful result. It is a good idea to research the market thoroughly – obtain brochures and visit showrooms and other outlets to gain a full appreciation of the different ranges available. Visiting a showroom allows you to stand at a sink, sit on a toilet and perhaps lie in a bathtub to assess whether such fixtures are comfortable for your height and frame.

Wall-hung sinks and toilets are more space-enhancing than pedestal versions because floor area is kept clear

■ Many bathroom manufacturers produce compact fixtures for small bathrooms. Bear in mind, however, that there is a limit to how far such fixtures can be miniaturized without compromising practicality.

■ Shaped fittings can also be space-saving. Tapered bathtubs, available in left- or right-hand versions, may allow you to position a tub across the width of the space rather than on the longest wall, which can free up the layout considerably. Sinks come in all shapes, including round, oval, square and rectangular.

■ Both sinks and toilets are available in corner versions, which can help make the most of floor area.

■ Wall-hung sinks and toilets are more space-enhancing than pedestal versions because the floor area is kept clear. You need to make sure the wall can bear the weight – such fixtures can be heavy and so require substantial anchoring. The water tanks of wall-hung toilets are concealed behind a dummy panel, which provides the perfect opportunity for built-in storage.

■ Coordinate the style and color of bathroom fixtures – if you are choosing porcelain fixtures, you cannot go wrong with white.

2

Bathrooms

Wet rooms

An emerging trend in bathroom design is the wet room, a fully waterproofed area where the shower drains directly to the floor. Converting a bathroom into a wet room makes good sense if the space is small, awkwardly shaped or both. Because fixtures are generally restricted to a sink and toilet and the shower is not enclosed by a cubicle or, indeed, screened in any way, floor area is maximized. When space is tight, it is difficult to prevent spray from a power shower from wetting everything within range; a fully waterproofed wet room sidesteps the problem altogether. Bathtubs can be sited within wet rooms if space permits.

1 A narrow wet room clad in tilework features a glass panel at the rear that makes the space feel less enclosed.
2 A shower draining directly to the floor is minimally separated from the rest of the bathroom by a glass screen. A skylight over the shower brings natural light down into the space.

3 Gridded wooden panels serve as the flooring of a wet room. When the panels are lifted up a sunken bathtub is revealed.
4 Another combination of wet room and bathroom is divided by a wooden partition. The tub is clad in mosaic tiles, while the wet room side features etched glass flooring.

Converting a bathroom into a wet room makes good sense if the space is small, awkwardly shaped or both

■ The floor should be laid so that water will run away readily to the drain and will not remain lying on the surface. Flooring materials should be as non-slip as possible.

■ Changes of level can help define different areas within a wet room.

■ Water pressure is a key consideration. Power showers require a certain degree of water pressure to work effectively. Thermostatic controls are essential if young children will be using the shower, as they enable water temperature to be set at a safe and comfortable level.

■ Wall-hung sinks and toilets accentuate the minimal qualities of the wet room.

■ Underfloor heating is ideal for wet rooms – and makes them even more pleasant to use – but it must be installed by a qualified electrician to prevent any risk of water coming into contact with the electrical supply.

■ Wet rooms do not lend themselves to storage: even towels positioned well away from the shower can get damp.

Waterproofing

The requirement for full waterproofing poses several constraints. You will need to clad the space in dense materials such as stone or tile, which may impose extra loads on the existing floor structure. Check with an architect or structural engineer to determine whether the floor will need to be strengthened. The ideal subfloor for a wet room is concrete, because it will not move in the way that wooden floor structures are prone to do, and therefore there is less risk of cracking and water penetration.

Surface cladding on its own, however, is not enough to provide full protection. The underlying wall and floor structure may well require additional waterproofing to make sure there is no risk that water might seep in and damage the structure of your home. This can be done in several different ways. "Tanking" consists of applying a bituminous layer or polyethylene membrane to the walls and floors before final finishes; sometimes the walls and floor are also lined in marine ply.

Bathrooms

Space-enhancing ideas

Clever ideas and spatial tricks will help you make the most of the area available and create a bathroom that is pleasant to use, rather than one that constantly reminds you of its shortcomings. Small changes made at the outset can help transform a potentially awkward space into an efficient and functional one.

Doors and partitions

■ Consider replacing a door that opens inward with a sliding panel or screen. Bifold or sliding shower screens also save space, as do sliding panels that provide access to concealed storage.

■ Semi-transparent doors or partitions increase the feeling of spaciousness by bringing natural light into the interior. Frosted glass preserves privacy; high-tech glass is also available that changes from opaque to clear at the flick of a switch.

■ Circular or semi-circular partitions enclosing a bathroom or wet room can make for a more dynamic use of space.

Decorating

■ Keep decoration simple and try to coordinate colors and materials. Color is not ruled out: in fact, when your home is restricted in size, a colorful bathroom can provide a welcome accent of vitality and interest. A single color, however, is enough.

■ Mirrors are an invaluable way of enhancing the sense of space. Position a mirror opposite an entrance or window, or line facing walls with mirrors to add width to the space.

■ Reflective surfaces and finishes – stainless steel, glazed tile and glass – bounce the light around.

■ Always extend tiling from floor to ceiling, leaving no awkward margins or gaps.

■ Pay particular attention to detailing. Junctions between materials or different finishes should be as neat and inconspicuous as possible.

1 A wall completely transformed into concealed storage houses bathroom necessities out of sight. Press-catches keep the effect neat and unobtrusive.
2 Bathroom fixtures come in a variety of shapes and sizes to enable you to cater for small or restricted layouts. This small circular wall-hung sink has wall-mounted taps. The mirrored wall behind serves as a shower screen for the tub.
3 A wall-mounted heated towel rail provides sufficient background heating to warm a small bathroom. The mirrors conceal built-in storage.
4 A toilet is concealed under a hinged lid within a stepped storage unit.
5 Open shelving and cubicles make good storage spaces for those items that you do not mind having on display, such as bath towels.

Services & fixtures

- Underfloor heating is particularly space-saving; alternatively, opt for a slimline wall-hung radiator.
- In a small bathroom a heated towel rail may be enough to heat the area to a comfortable temperature.
- Taps fixed to the wall reduce visual clutter; monomixers take up less space than a pair of taps.
- An efficient exhaust fan is essential, regardless of whether the bathroom has a window or not.

Lighting

- Top lighting in the form of skylights can dramatically enhance the sense of volume in a restricted space.
- Bathtubs and vanity units that are faced in backlit translucent panels appear much less bulky than their solid counterparts and produce an atmospheric ambient light.
- Tiny spots or downlights recessed into the ceiling around the perimeter of the room will increase the feeling of spaciousness, as will concealed lighting in the corners of the room or at the junction of the ceiling and walls.

Storage

- Keep visual clutter to a minimum. Restrict what is out on view to essential items only – such as towels, soap and toothbrushes.
- Take the opportunity to build in storage wherever possible, underneath sinks, between sinks and toilets or at either end of the bathtub.

Keep visual clutter to a minimum; restrict what is out on view to essential items only – such as towels, soap and toothbrushes

4

5

Home Office

Incorporating a work area into your home can pose quite a challenge when every last square foot is seemingly already accounted for, but it is not impossible, given a little forethought and ingenuity. Much, however, will depend on the nature of the work in question. Working from home all or part of the time is a demographic trend that shows no signs of abating. If you are a one-person operation and your work is largely computer-based or desk-bound, setting up a compact home office should not be too difficult. If you employ staff, or if your work entails regular visits from clients or suppliers, or makes particular demands in terms of specialized equipment or storage of supplies and finished goods, you are not going to be able to accommodate your business within a small domestic setup. Either you will have to rent studio or office space, consider converting an attic or basement for the purpose (see pages 96–109) or investigate the possibility of making use of an addition, outbuilding or shed (see pages 118–123).

1 In a small space you may not necessarily want your home office on view all the time. This arrangement, where an angled panel slides forward on casters to reveal a work station, maintains a degree of separation from the rest of the household.

Siting

Assuming that what you chiefly require is a work station of some sort, the main decision is where to site it. Even if you live alone or work mainly during the day when no one else is at home, a work area should still provide some psychological separation from daily life, which will aid your concentration and self-discipline. Ideally, you should also be able to leave work in progress without having to tidy everything away at the end of the day; if that is not possible, which it may well not be, at least try to position your desk where there is a minimum of disruption and where you will not be distracted by the comings and goings of the rest of the household (and vice versa).

Options for siting include

- Near or in front of a window in a living area, kitchen or bedroom – a view is a powerful aid to concentration. A bay window, which provides an element of enclosure and a wider spread of natural light, can be a good position.
- On a generous-sized landing. Top lighting from a skylight can help enhance the sense of space.
- Tucked into an understairs area.
- On a loft or platform level, provided head room is sufficient.
- Discreetly built into a working wall of storage. Many efficient and compact home offices are integrated into concealed storage areas. With shelves above for storing work-related files and a pull-out surface to serve as a desktop, this type of arrangement is ideal for multipurpose spaces. Make sure lighting is adequate and allows you to see your computer screen with ease.

Live-work

When redundant industrial, commercial and retail premises first began to be converted into desirable urban lofts, many planners were reluctant to allow "change of use" unless some employment-generating element was retained on site. Nowadays, attitudes have relaxed somewhat and many conversions of old buildings, as well as some new developments, are now specifically marketed as "live-work" units.

"Live-work," however, is more specific in its implications than the rather amorphous concept of "working from home." If you choose to purchase or rent a live-work unit, for example, you may well find that regulations stipulate how much of the overall space should be used for working (which may be as high as 50 percent), as well as the type of business that is permitted. Other restrictions will also apply to ensure that your business does not affect your neighbors adversely in terms of noise, increased traffic and other environmental considerations. It is also important to check out the financial implications, particularly with respect to taxes and utilies.

The work environment

A home office should be furnished and equipped so that you can work efficiently and productively, and, above all, at no long-term risk to your health. Compared with careers such as firefighting, where the risks of personal injury are self-evident, desk

One of the best investments you can make is to buy yourself an ergonomic task chair

1 An alcove in a living area has been outfitted as a compact home office space, complete with storage drawers, open shelving and a work surface. A translucent glass screen slides across when the home office is not in use.

2 If you are going to be running a business from home, you will need a dedicated work area where you will be able to separate yourself from the rest of the household and leave work in progress, without having to tidy everything away at the end of the day.

3 How you set up your home office/work area will depend to a large extent on the nature of your work. A drawing board and an adjustable light, along with shelving for reference books and files, are suitable for creative work.

4 A home office at its most minimal – a hinged panel on casters, just deep enough to provide room for a laptop, desk light and a few box files.

3

4

work may not seem to present any particular hazards. However, many people find their working lives compromised through back pain, RSI (repetitive strain injury), eye strain and other forms of work-related stress. Working from home can actually increase the risk of such injuries and illnesses, particularly if you opt for an ad hoc arrangement and do not take the time to choose furniture or equipment that has been ergonomically designed for the job. Working at the kitchen table may be adequate if all you are going to be doing is paying a few bills and balancing your checkbook; if you are likely to be sitting for long hours compiling a report, you need a work surface that is the right height and a chair that has been designed for office use.

Wireless technology

The arrival of wireless technology enables you to set up a home network, so that every computer in your house can access the Internet at the same time, print using the same printer, scan using the same scanner and so on. In turn, this means you can position the printer and scanner away from the main work area, provided the signal is strong enough in the chosen location.

■ **Chair** One of the best investments you can make when setting up a home office is to buy an ergonomic task chair. Specifically designed to prevent the most common side effect of prolonged sedentary work, namely back pain, such chairs are not cheap but should last a long time. Features to look out for include a padded, tiltable seat with a rounded front edge, adjustable height and a curved, tiltable back rest.

■ **Work surface** If you are using a computer, you will need staggered levels of work surface, with a lower level for the keyboard, a middle level for general desk work and a higher level for the screen.

■ **Lighting** Good natural light is essential for most concentrated work and for work where making fine color judgments is important. In terms of artificial light, overall levels should be up to four times the light level that is comfortable for relaxation. Computer work requires slightly less because the screen is lit. Use uplighters to give background illumination; supplement with directional task lighting to light the keyboard or read documents.

■ **Storage** You will need three distinct levels of storage: storage close at hand to keep immediate supplies and work in progress; storage at one remove for reference, recent projects and backup supplies; and deep storage for documentation relating to your work history, as well as tax returns and accounts.

Small Yards

Any outdoor space, however limited in size, can make a huge difference to your enjoyment of life – somewhere to sit out and eat on warm days, a place to nurture favorite flowers and plants, a soothing green enclave that reminds you of nature amid the harshest urban environment.

In less densely populated parts of the world, what counts as a small yard is likely to be much more generous than a city-dweller's definition of "small." Increasingly, however, land is at such a premium that many would-be gardeners find themselves with a smaller space to play with than they would have liked. But even the tiniest, most unpromising spaces can be transformed into veritable oases using a little creativity and ingenuity. And if you do not have a yard, what about a balcony, roof deck or the windowsills?

As far as inspiration is concerned, it is not necessary or always helpful to base your ideas on famous garden schemes – the Monticellos, Sissinghurts and Butchart Gardens. Simply look around in your neighborhood for those sights that make you smile – the wisteria twining up the front of a cottage, the cheery pots of geraniums flanking a doorstep, the shaded garden bench in an ivy-clad courtyard. Like good cooking, good gardening is often about simple ideas done well.

1

1 A combination of different materials – gravel, decking and stone slabs – adds inherent vitality to a small yard. Lawns rarely earn their keep when outdoor space is very restricted in size.

Assessing your outdoor space

The first step in the process of creating a successful small yard – indeed, any yard – is a thorough assessment, both of what you have to work with and of what your needs are. A small yard is not simply defined by scale; there may be other limitations to take into account. Working with, rather than against, these will achieve the best result.

■ **Light and shade** Which areas in the yard get the sun and at what times of the day? You cannot do much about the basic orientation of your yard, but you can ameliorate extreme conditions to some extent. Noting the sunny places will give you ideas about where to site seating areas as well as where to plant sun-loving species. If your yard is very shady or hemmed in by tall buildings, as is the case with many urban back yards, you will need to plan your planting accordingly.

■ **Soil conditions** Use a testing kit to determine what type of soil you have in your yard. Poor soil can be improved to some extent by drainage, adding fresh topsoil and digging in organic matter, but basic ground conditions will affect which plants are likely to do best and which will not thrive. Neighboring gardens – or the surrounding landscape – can give you a clue about soil type. You can control soil in containers quite easily and economically.

■ **Exposure** Note the direction of the prevailing wind. How sheltered is your yard from the elements? Fencing, trellising and other barriers can help provide better conditions and protect delicate plants.

■ **Personal requirements** How much time and money are you prepared to devote to the project? How much maintenance do you want to put in on a daily, weekly or seasonal basis?

Small Yards

1 When you are planning the layout of your yard, think about basic practicalities, such as where you are going to store tools, pots and other equipment. This lidded wooden bin, built up against a fence, makes for useful tool storage and doubles up as a table or additional seating.

2 Small yards appear even smaller when you are able to see them at a single glance. This family yard is not extensive in size, but the arrangement of separate areas for dining, relaxed seating and play effectively breaks up the space into a series of outdoor rooms.

Planning and layout

Planning a yard, like planning an interior space, begins on paper. Before you start the design process, measure your space, draw a sketch plan and note existing features, particularly those you wish to retain. You can also mark on any boundaries – walls, fencing and so on – that require repair or replacement. Then use the measurements and sketch plan to make a scale drawing (see page 23). One of the great advantages of a small yard is that it is easier to design on paper at a workable scale.

A camera can also be useful in the planning process. Take pictures from the back of the yard, looking toward the house, and vice versa, as well as from side to side, so that you can begin to think in terms of views and vistas.

In a small yard your aim should be to make the most of available space. This does not mean trying to find a way to cram everything in – the result will be a cluttered and claustrophobic place that provides little tranquillity and respite. Before you concern yourself with what type of yard you would like to create – its mood, style and appearance, and even the planting – think about function and practicality, in order to allocate space effectively and get the basic structure of the yard right. Try to think in terms of priorities – a small yard will not be able to fulfil every conceivable need, so which is most important to you? If your outside space is very small, you may be able to satisfy only one or two requirements effectively, but that is much better than attempting to meet every need and serving none well.

1

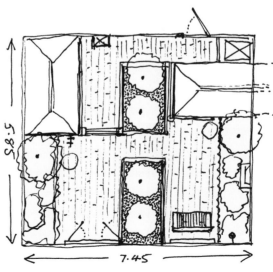

2

Before deciding on a style for your yard, think about function and practicality in order to allocate space effectively and get the basic structure of the garden right

■ **Seating area** Do you want somewhere to sit and enjoy the yard? Where would such a seating area be best located? Will shading or shelter be required?

■ **Eating area** Eating – and cooking – outdoors is a great pleasure. If you like to barbecue, you might consider devoting space to a built-in grill.

■ **Growing your own** Would you like to grow your own fruit, vegetables, herbs or flowers? Even the tiniest windowsill garden can still provide room for pots of fresh herbs.

■ **Play area** How much of your yard will be given over to children's play? Do your children simply need space to let off steam and kick a ball, or are they clamoring for play equipment, such as swing sets and trampolines?

■ **Ancillary needs** Do you want a shed or greenhouse? Is there room for a compost heap? Do you need to keep your recycling or garbage bins in the yard, as is generally the case with areas or yards at the front of the house?

Small Yards

Design principles

Once you have roughly decided how much of your outside space to devote to different activities, it is time to begin the process of design. Again, working it out on paper first will help you see the big picture without becoming distracted by existing planting or garden features.

Simplicity

One of the most important principles of successful small yard design is simplicity. By simplicity I do not mean minimalism, I mean coming up with one or two strong ideas or concepts and avoiding unnecessary clutter. Gardens that are overgrown, that resemble a nursery catalog run riot or where there are too many incidental features warring with one another are visually distracting. As is the case with interior design, points of interest require sufficient breathing space to be appreciated fully.

Themes and unifiers include:

■ A chosen style – for example, a Japanese-inspired courtyard garden.
■ One strong or dominant feature – a pool, an arch, a piece of garden furniture or sculpture.
■ Yards whose impact chiefly rests on architectural or foliage plants, or where planting is restricted to a massing of several species to provide drifts of color.
■ A relatively restricted palette of surfaces and finishes.

Gardens that are overgrown or where there are too many incidental features warring with one another are visually distracting

1 Wooden decking and furniture provide a strong unifying element on a rooftop deck. When the space is very small, focus on a single activity – in this case outdoor dining – rather than attempt to cater to a range of different needs.
2 A narrow lightwell is planted with bamboo set in trough containers on a gravel bed – a very effective and low-maintenance scheme.
3 Containerized plants and a small tree dapple the light in a small paved back yard. Fewer, larger specimens are better than too many small plants dotted around.
4 Rules are made to be broken. This tiny yard has been planted with overscale species to create a miniature urban jungle.

The foundation of any yard is a strong framework, expressed in the dynamic interrelation of different shapes and volumes. The starting point, of course, is the shape of the yard itself, but there are many ways in which you can overcome apparent limitations through thoughtful design.

One of the worst ways of approaching small yard design is to run narrow beds up the sides and along the back, leaving the greater proportion of the space grassed or paved. This timid, tentative approach results in a flat, dead area that seems appended, rather than connected, to indoor areas. A further disadvantage is that any interest supplied by the planting will be largely invisible from indoors. Rather than making the most of available space, this strategy actually makes a small yard seem smaller, because boundaries are obvious and the entire space can be viewed in a single glance.

All yards will seem more spacious if everything is not revealed at once, if they invite discovery and offer surprise. The tried-and-true strategy in this respect is to subdivide the yard into different "rooms" or areas and connect them in such a way as to make use of every corner. In this way the eye is tricked into believing that the yard extends further than it really does. In small yards the areas will necessarily be smaller and the connections shorter, but the same principle holds.

You can lay out such areas in a formal way, with strong geometric shapes, such as squares, rectangles and circles, or more informally, using curves and more organically shaped areas. Alternatively, a well-judged mixture of the two can be very effective.

Once you have plotted different areas on paper, try out the effect in the yard itself using temporary divisions or screens, or by roughing out shapes on the ground using string stretched between pegs. This will help you think three-dimensionally and envisage the garden as a series of contrasting volumes.

Small Yards

Views, vistas and focal points

The whole point about laying out a yard as a sequence of spaces is to invite discovery and provide richness of experience. For such an arrangement to be fully effective, you need to consider both views and focal points. Views draw the eye onward, suggesting that there is more to be explored; focal points lend coherence and stability to a design, which helps hold different elements together in balance.

Always consider the views from your home out on to the yard and vice versa. Both aspects should provide a sense of delight and encourage movement and progression from one area to the other. The view that you frame may not be in your yard at all: "borrowed" views, of a neighboring tree, for example, can be very enticing.

Many small urban yards, especially those that are overlooked by neighboring buildings, offer little scope for tantalizing views – in fact, rather the reverse, as there may well be unappealing sights that you wish to screen out. In this case the best approach is to provide simple, clear internal focal points – an overscaled container or urn, for example, or a garden seat or sculpture.

My most successful urban garden was at the back of a townhouse in London. I made two large circles of brick paving stones, which I joined where they touched in the center. Planting was around the edges of the circles, furthest away from the house. You could look down on the garden from the upper floor of the house and it looked very calm and sculptural.

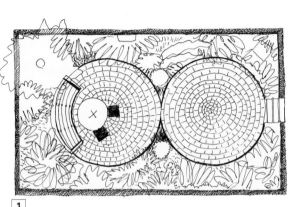

1

3

2

Paths and connections

We naturally like to take the shortest distance between two points, as evidenced in those shortcuts tracked across parks where paths go the long way around. In a garden you need to strike a balance between connecting different areas directly (the practical approach) and taking what one might call the scenic route (the aesthetic approach).

■ Paths should be laid in the areas that will see the most wear, otherwise you will find bare patches in your lawn or your flowerbeds will be trodden down. The point where you enter your yard and the routes between its main elements should be connected with paving or surfaced in some other hard-wearing material.

■ If your yard is very narrow, laying paving stones or bricks widthwise will make it seem wider than it is.

1 The plan of one of my yards in London. The design was based on two large brick circles that met in the center of the space, with planting around the edges.

2 An archway frames a view beyond the eating area, leading the eye onward and creating an illusion of greater space.

3 Recycled materials are cobbled together to create a charming urban oasis.

4 A curved path can make a small yard seem bigger than it is, because the whole space is not revealed at once or from a single viewpoint.

■ If your garden is short, bricks or paving stones laid end to end will make paths seem longer.

■ Materials that are small in scale, such as cobblestone or gravel, increase the sense of space.

■ Slight variations in level – a few steps up or down – add a sense of vitality to yard connections.

Surfaces and materials

In small gardens much of the interest may derive from your choice of surfaces and materials. Although many people find it hard to resist the default mode of grass when it comes to laying out main garden areas, minuscule areas of lawn are never very effective and demand disproportionate amounts of maintenance for the aesthetic benefits they offer. It is often better to pave the greater portion of a small garden using a sympathetic combination of different materials.

Always consider the setting and the architectural character of your home when choosing garden materials. Decking and paths made of railway ties are sympathetic choices for wood houses; flagstone and brick work well in country locations; contemporary, urban choices include bricks, plain stone slabs, gravel paths and washed beach pebbles.

Small Yards

Connecting home and garden

In good weather even a small yard has the potential to become an alfresco living room or eating area. Equally valuable, especially when your home is limited in size, is to make sure your living space visually extends to incorporate the garden, deck, balcony or patio adjacent to it. With the right design and decorative choices, the yard will be seen as a seamless continuation of the indoor areas. Improving the connection between indoors and out is an important strategy for enhancing spatial quality overall.

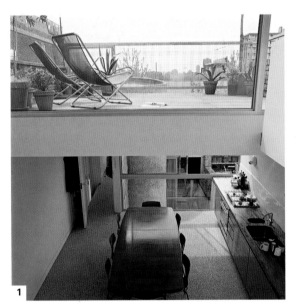

1 Take advantage of outdoor space wherever you find it – at the front of your home, to the side or rear, or above. This roof deck has been laid out very simply with a few containerized plants and a couple of deck chairs.
2 Glazed double doors lead directly on to a shaded deck for eating. Wooden flooring indoors is echoed by the decking outside.
3 Pure white rendered concrete makes a formal backdrop for a minimally planted contemporary yard.

Points to consider

■ Views Dissolving the boundary between indoors and outdoors may entail creating new openings or enlarging existing ones. Replacing a window with a door, French doors or floor-to-ceiling sliding glass doors immediately brings the outside world a little closer. If access to the yard is limited to a back door in a hallway or kitchen, consider ways of improving access and views from the main living area (see pages 36–9).

■ Flooring and paving Matching materials indoors and out underscores the sense of connection between the house and garden. You may not wish to replicate the same surface outdoors for reasons of cost or practicality, but materials that are similar in tone or texture will create the same effect equally well.

■ Areas of transition The entrance to the yard and the area immediately adjacent to the house lends itself to being treated as an outdoor seating or eating area. If possible, the patio should extend the width of the house and far enough out into the yard to fit a table and chairs or benches comfortably. This transitional area can then be framed with soft plantings, low walls or similar forms of enclosure to frame the garden beyond.

■ Lighting Sensitive garden and patio lighting is not only highly evocative, it also allows outdoor areas to be used during the evening. Low lights, uplights and flares are more sympathetic than high-level lighting and less likely to annoy neighbors or contribute to light pollution. Always consult a qualified electrician when it comes to installing external lighting circuits. All outdoor wiring should be fitted with a circuit breaker; control switches should be located inside the house.

■ Outdoor walls Garden walls can be constructed, rendered and decorated so that they match interior walls and thus lead the eye onward. In the case of kitchens directly connecting to outdoor spaces, you can also extend work surfaces or counters to form an unbroken line from indoors to out. The space underneath can be used to store garden tools, toys and deck chairs.

■ Furniture Where garden areas are outdoor rooms, pay particular attention to the style of furniture, so that there are no abrupt contrasts with the type of pieces you are using indoors.

3

Small Yards

Front yards

If most or all of your available outdoor space is at the front of the house, it is unlikely that you will want to use it for those activities – such as lazing on a deck chair in the sun or having a family barbecue – for which most people demand the privacy of a back yard. Front yards are, by virtue of their location, semi-public spaces, open to the view of passersby, whether on foot or in cars. Crime is also an issue: in these security-conscious days, obscuring planting may well serve as a buffer to prying eyes, but it also provides an all-too-convenient screen for intruders intent on burglary.

Other practical limitations include the fact that front yards are often where containers for recycling or garbage are located – which, in turn, may attract scavenging cats and dogs. You may also require a hard, level surface for parking; or the garden may directly abut a driveway.

Practical considerations notwithstanding, there is every reason to plan and plant a front yard with as much care and consideration as a yard in the rear of the property. Attractive front gardens frame and enhance the entrance to your home, spell out a message of welcome and brighten up the neighborhood considerably.

Points to consider

■ Keep planting, hedges and boundary walls low, so that your home can be viewed clearly from the street.
■ Small specimen trees can be attractive, but choose the species with care. Trees that grow too tall will block out natural light, while those whose root systems are too extensive can undermine the foundations of your home and may affect public sidewalks.
■ Illuminate front paths and entrance doors so that both you and your visitors can navigate the way safely after dark. Motion-sensitive lighting is a proven deterrent to burglars.

1

1 Relatively low planting creates a welcoming sight at the front of the house while not obscuring the entrance or compromising security.
2 Planters and containers come in a vast range of materials. These wooden planters blend in well with the wood decking.
3 Galvanized aluminum buckets make handsome containers for plants with spiky foliage.

2   3

Plants grown in containers, rather than planted directly in the ground, are the mainstay of small space gardening

■ Climbers and creepers can be trained up facing walls to soften elevations.

■ Shrubs and ground cover are better choices than lawns for small front yards.

■ Screen garbage containers with plants or construct shelters.

■ A pair of containerized plants on each side of the front door creates an inviting feel. Vary the planting according to the seasons.

Container gardening

Plants grown in containers, rather than planted directly in the ground, are the mainstay of small space gardening. You can position containers in front areas, in small paved back courtyards, or on patios, balconies, windowsills and roof gardens.

Points to consider

■ Plant containers with species that will survive the conditions to which you will expose them. This is of particular importance for roof decks, which are usually very open to the elements.

■ Large containers, filled with soil and well watered, can be very heavy. If you are placing pots, troughs, urns or window boxes on balconies or roofs, make sure the surface can bear the load.

■ Container gardening is not maintenance-free. You will need to water frequently during the warm months, which means it is important to site containers near a convenient outdoor water supply, unless you are prepared to make many trips in and out of the house.

■ Containers come in a wide range of materials, from wood, zinc and terracotta to unlovely plastic or fiberglass (only for those containers not intended to be seen). You can also improvise quirky containers from empty olive-oil cans and other recycled items.

Small Yards

Roof gardens

One type of small garden that poses particular challenges is the roof garden. Exposure, weight, drainage and security are some of the issues that need to be addressed to create a successful rooftop oasis. The effort is worth it: roof gardens, with their sweeping views, are enchanting outdoor spaces.

1 High above street level, pink flamingos and planters adapted from soft-drink crates add a quirky touch to a roof patio.
2 Open to the elements. On nice days this glazed roof can be slid back to bring light and air down into the interior. The remainder of the roof is given over to an outdoor patio.

3 A Japanese-style garden on the roof makes use of the basic elements of decking, gravel, stones and low containerized shrubs.

Points to consider

■ **Roof structure** You will need to consult a structural engineer to determine whether the existing roof structure is strong enough to bear the additional load of containerized plants, paving, waterproofing and draining layers. In some cases it may be possible to support decking on parapet walls to lighten the load on the roof and provide an attractive surface.

■ **Waterproofing and drainage** The roof must be fully waterproofed to prevent moisture from seeping into the roof structure and causing damage. Plants should be grown in containers or tanks filled with lightweight aggregates under a shallow layer of compost to promote free drainage. A rooftop water tank is useful for irrigation.

■ **Exposure** A rooftop location often means exposure to full sunlight and wind, so choose plants that flourish in dry climates. Wind can also be a problem. Semi-permeable screens, such as trellis, bamboo, canvas or wire mesh, provide a better means of sheltering plantings than solid barriers that can set up wind turbulence.

■ **Security** Some form of enclosure will be necessary for safety. Consult your local planning department and building inspector for recommended guidelines. Never leave children unattended on a roof garden.

■ **Living roofs** If you do not want to use a roof garden as an additional outdoor living space, you can still green your roof by planting it with grasses and wildflowers. Living roofs, which are a common vernacular feature in areas of Europe, have been widely adopted by eco builders. The vegetation helps insulate the house, replaces the area of ground lost to construction and helps to balance carbon dioxide emissions.

3

Second Homes & Weekend Retreats

Size is often less of an issue when it comes to second homes and weekend retreats. Second homes rarely have to cater to the full range of activities that a main place of residence necessarily must do; then again, an element of camping out is all part of the experience of getting away from it all. Unless you are maintaining a basic pied-à-terre in the city for the working week and repairing to a country home at weekends to do most of your "living," spatial limitations will be less of a drawback. In fact, larger properties can pose their own difficulties in terms of upkeep and running costs. If you will be occupying the place only for short periods, it is generally more cost-effective and less time-consuming if it is compact and, hence, easy and cheap to run.

While a second home provides the opportunity to recharge in less hectic surroundings, the experience of living simply can also instruct us in how to remove the clutter and complexity from our everyday lives. Small space living, at home or away, has the potential to concentrate the mind on what is truly essential and help us reassess priorities to gain more enjoyment from life.

1 An A-line chalet makes a perfect retreat in skiing country. The acute slope of the roof is designed to shrug off deep snowfalls.

The location of your main home may have been determined by a number of prosaic factors: proximity to work or school, budget, transport links and the like. Superficially, it may well seem that deciding where to spend your free time will be less restricted by such mundane issues and will be more likely to be influenced by personal preferences – a desire to be near the sea, for example, or a lifelong ambition to own a place in France. Nevertheless, it is crucial not to neglect the practicalities.

Points to consider

■ **Distance** The closer your second home is to your first home, or the easier it is to travel there, the more likely you are to use it. Distance is not measurable simply in miles, however. Frequent cheap flights can mean that remote areas are quicker to get to and more accessible than places that you can reach only after hours of sitting in gridlocked traffic with all the other weekenders.

■ **Local character** Make sure you do your research and find out what the area is like out of season, especially if you intend to spend weekends there throughout the year, rather than a period in summer or winter. Are there places to visit or things to do when the weather is less than ideal? Are there stores within a reasonable distance where you can stock up on necessities? Is there transportation or will you be reliant on a car?

■ **Short-term renting** Is the location popular with tourists? If so, you may have a better chance of renting out your second home during those periods when you will not be using it.

■ **Legalities** When buying or renting abroad, make sure you understand local codes and regulations. Notary fees, for example, can add 10 percent to the purchase price of a property in parts of Europe.

Second Homes & Weekend Retreats

1 Second homes in the country often benefit from a more relaxed approach to decoration and furnishing – a back-to-basics setting will help get you in the mood for relaxation.

2 A simple cabin raised up on concrete piers minimizes disruption to the site in unspoiled countryside. Many prefab and eco designs are now available if you want to build your own cottage or weekend retreat.

3 A cabin in the woods is simply furnished with stained wood walls, homespun blankets and plenty of reading material.

4 A pair of bunk beds built into the fabric of the room provides sleeping space for all the children. The white and blue color scheme echoes the maritime setting.

Expressing a sense of place

Many people opt for a second home as a way of connecting with nature or as a means of enjoying a stunning setting away from the hustle and bustle of the city. Whether your retreat is a ski lodge, a seaside cottage, a lakeside cabin or a converted barn in the middle of unspoiled countryside, reinforcing a sense of place and reflecting the immediate context should inform your design decisions when it comes to choosing materials for renovation and decoration.

One way to achieve this is to make use of local materials. This is particularly important when it comes to renovating, converting or restoring older properties, such as farmhouses, cottages, barns and stables. Local regulations will often stipulate what

you can do, in any case, particularly if alterations will affect the external appearance of the building. If you are building a new home, using a dominant local material can make a contemporary design blend in with its setting more successfully.

Views and vistas bring nature closer to home. Planning regulations often do not allow you to alter elevations significantly; if you are renovating a period cottage, you may not be able to enlarge existing windows. In this case taking down some internal partitions can help lighten and brighten the interior (see pages 36–41). Alternatively, you could explore the possibility of adding on a glass extension to dissolve the boundary between indoors and out (see pages 110–17).

Decor and furnishings

There is no law that says that just because your second home is located in the country you have to adopt a rustic or countrified decorating scheme, or slip back a century or two in your choice of furnishings to reflect the age of the property. Spare, contemporary interiors can be very successful, particularly as they are generally easier to maintain than more fussy styles; they also promote the relaxed lifestyle that is what a second home should be all about.

■ Natural surfaces and finishes, such as wooden floors, terracotta tiles and exposed brick or stonework, can take a fair amount of punishment and still age well. Cheap synthetics will only degrade rapidly.

■ Using pale colors or plenty of white in your decorating scheme will help enhance levels of natural light and spread it around as much as possible.
■ Choose flexible furniture that allows you to put up and entertain visitors as required with minimal upheaval: sofa beds or divans, folding or stacking chairs and extendable tables.
■ Keep soft furnishings simple, washable and strong enough to withstand wear and tear.
■ Avoid using your second home as a repository for cast-offs. You do not need to furnish a weekend or vacation home expensively, but it will not be a pleasant or restorative place to visit if it is filled with mismatched pieces or items that you would otherwise want to get rid of.

Second Homes & Weekend Retreats

Practicalities

The degree to which you enjoy your second home and, potentially, the ease with which you will be able to rent it out, if that is your intention, will also depend on which systems of organization you put in place. Second homes are double the trouble if they do not, to a certain extent, look after themselves.

1 A canvas awning strung up between two cabins screens an outdoor eating area. Large hurricane lamps supply atmospheric lighting and are practical in breezy weather.
2 A basic kitchen features a pair of gas rings powered by liquid petroleum gas and simple cooking equipment stowed on shelves screened by wire mesh. Make sure your cooking facilities actually work – there is a fine line between camping out and roughing it.
3 The perennial favorite, the beach house or hut, provides a water's-edge view of the ocean and a convenient retreat on wet days.

3

- Even if you do not intend to rent out your second home, make sure you fully equip it with necessary household items, so that you do not waste time and energy transporting cooking equipment or vacuum cleaners back and forth.
- Buying toilet paper, garbage bags, light bulbs and other basic provisions in bulk will help ensure you are never caught short when you arrive in the dead of night. A well-stocked freezer can also be useful if you have the space.
- Provide decent cooking facilities – a stove that really works and is reliable, not one that is on its last legs. Kitchens can be basic, but they must function properly.
- Make sure the property is thoroughly secured when it is not occupied. Installing security or alarm systems and advising neighbors to keep a lookout when you are away can help prevent break-ins. It can be helpful to seek the advice of local police or crime prevention officers.
- If your property includes extensive grounds, you may wish to hire a local gardener to keep it in order. You might also hire someone local to inspect the property from time to time to spot any potential problems, such as a leaking roof or a blocked drain.

- If you are financing your second home by renting it out for periods of the year, make sure you consult a financial advisor so that you are fully informed about how this affects your tax position.
- Rentals can be organized through agents, who can also be retained to troubleshoot any problems that arise. Otherwise, you may wish to rely on your wider net of friends and family, advertise in an alumni bulletin or in-house newsletter or post the details of the rental (including recent photographs) on the Internet.
- Make sure you are fully insured for damage and breakages. If you are renting out your second home, do not leave anything at the property that has real or sentimental value.
- Keep instructions for operating appliances in an accessible location. Useful details and information, including emergency telephone numbers, bus timetables and the opening hours of local attractions, should always be prominently displayed.

**Provide decent cooking facilities,
such as a stove that really works,
not one that is on its last legs –
kitchens can be basic, but they
must function properly**

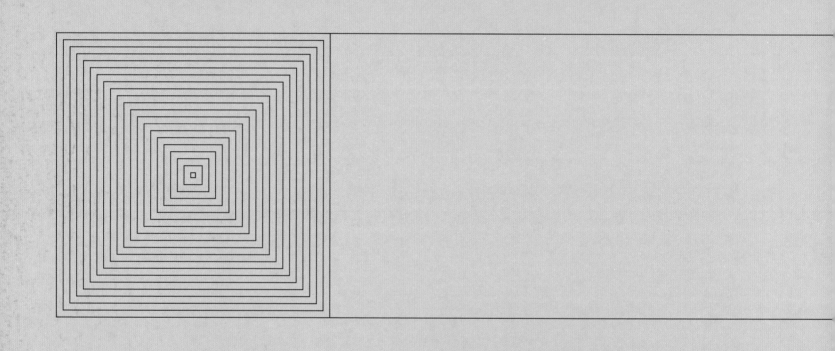

Case Study
3773 studio project, Los Angeles, CA

What Studio and bathroom converted from two-car garage.

Where Mar Vista, Los Angeles, California, a residential area developed between the 1930s and 1950s.

Problem Extra space required for a home office, as well as flexible living accommodation and a bathroom. Conversion work must conform to local codes that require all houses to have two-car garages.

Goal To convert the existing 400 sq. ft. (37 m²) garage into 640 sq. ft. (59 m²) of studio space, with bathroom, loft and kitchen area, while conforming to building codes. To integrate internal and external spaces with new landscaping. Issues of recycling, sustainability and energy efficiency to inform the overall design.

Solution A flexible conversion of an existing two-car garage provides accommodation that can be configured in a number of ways. Use of recycled and sustainable materials and other "green" strategies produces a building of low environmental impact. The final stage will see the completion of a roof deck and garden formed by a "saddle" fitted to the roof parapet.

1

2

3

1 External view of the converted garage, with double Dutch doors. The bathroom to the right is also accessed by external doors.

2 The kitchen bay within the studio features a counter made of construction-grade lumber laminated together and sanded down to a smooth surface.

3 The main live-work space in the studio provides room for a home office as well as a living/dining area. The wooden "tray" suspended from the roof trusses is a sleeping platform.

Home studio

Those who find themselves short of space at home naturally start to look to existing outbuildings, sheds or garages with an eye for their conversion potential. In this case a 400 sq. ft. (37 m²) detached double garage seemed ideal for the purpose. The initial hurdle, however, was to come up with a scheme that satisfied local building codes.

In this particular area of Los Angeles, California, two-car detached garages are required by law for all homes – a requirement that has not prevented many ad hoc conversions from taking place. In many cases these garages are not used to house cars at all but become hobby rooms, workshops, storage areas and illegal living units. To meet building code requirements, the solution here was to provide large external Dutch doors, each wide enough to accommodate the width of a car so that the building could easily be converted back to its former use. The bathroom, which reads as a separate volume, is also accessed through external doors.

The conversion of the garage provides flexible accommodation for a home office or studio, along with a full bathroom, including indoor and outdoor showers. The space can also be used as a living area. A wooden "tray" suspended from the roof trusses provides a sleeping area, while there is also a kitchen bay with laundry facilities.

Green building practices and principles informed the design process. Elements of the old garage were reused in the new design, including large beams that

1 The double Dutch doors can be fully open or configured in different ways to aid natural ventilation and cool the interior. The floor construction is a concrete slab.
2 Internal view of the sleeping platform. The expressed structural beams and supports have a robust, lively integrity.

3 External landscaping reflects the need for water conservation in a naturally arid area. Decomposed granite and broken concrete for the driveway reduce the need for extensive lawns.

were remilled to provide structural supports. All structural and finish lumber is sustainable Douglas fir. Joists larger than 2 x 6 in. (5 x 15 cm) are "microlams," to avoid using large beams from older-growth trees. Internal wall finishes are made of "homosote" panels, composed of recycled newsprint, finished with beeswax and linseed oil. Construction-grade framing materials, laminated together and sanded down, form tables and counter surfaces.

Gas-fired wall heaters provide a radiant heat source in winter. The well-insulated ceiling, reflective roof coatings and cross-ventilation through Dutch doors and clerestory windows help cool the space in summer. Water drains from the new studio roof into a large bamboo planter that screens a neighboring

building and provides privacy for the outdoor shower. The outdoor shower also drains into the same planter.

The new landscaping was designed to integrate the two buildings on site in a natural way. As garages can be built right on the property line, unlike main houses, there was the opportunity to create a more dynamic courtyard to link the two buildings. Large areas of decomposed granite reduce the need for extensive areas of lawn, which make heavy demands on water use in an arid area.

The conversion of the garage provides flexible accommodation for a home office or studio with full bathroom and kitchen; the space can also be used as a living area

A Reflecting pool
B Garden planter
C Lawn
D Outdoor shower
E Bathroom
F Kitchen
G Access to loft
H Living area

Case Study
Live-work maisonette, London

What Live-work maisonette on three levels.
Where Hoxton, London
Problem Three-bedroom ex-council maisonette with poky rooms and a tiny bathroom, originally arranged over two levels. The property had not been decorated in 20 years.

Goal To open out the interior as much as possible. To renew and redecorate surfaces and finishes. To put in a new kitchen and a new bathroom. To provide as much concealed storage as possible. To create a separate area that could be used as a home office.

Solution Many of the internal walls were taken down to open up the existing space. The ceiling on the top floor was removed to open up into the attic void and a loft level was introduced. Materials and furnishings were chosen to be as space-enhancing as possible. As only one bedroom was required, the remaining space was reconfigured to provide a new generous-sized bathroom and a work area.

1 The main work area occupies the greater proportion of the second level, and runs from the front of the maisonette to the rear. Neutral carpeting is a good unifier.
2 The new loft level, created out of part of the attic void, is furnished with a plexiglass table and chair, which preserve sightlines. A narrow slit in the rear wall conceals strip lighting, which is colored by a red gel and washes the wall behind the freestanding storage unit with light.

Working from home

Occupying the top two floors of a four-story block in East London, this maisonette was originally laid out as a series of small, rather poky rooms, with the bathroom being particularly tiny. In addition, it had not been decorated for 20 years. The architect who bought the property required only one bedroom. What he did need was an office for his practice.

The chief strategy in structural terms was to remove internal walls and open up the spaces as much as possible. A narrow passage leading from the front door was extended into a former cupboard to give an L-shaped vestibule. A new opening was created between the kitchen and the main room on the lower floor, which became a combined dining and living area. Upstairs, on the second floor, all the walls were taken down except for those enclosing one bedroom, with the remainder of the space, which runs from the front of the house to the back, serving as a work area. The ceiling was also removed at this level to knock through into the attic void, creating a double-height space. To make room for an additional office, a new loft level was introduced, accessed by

The chief strategy in structural terms was to remove internal walls and open the spaces up as much as possible

3 A view from the bedroom to the work area. The monk's stairs to the loft are made of MDF and painted red.
4 The large chocolate-brown panel to the left of the work area can be slid across to separate the office from the bedroom. Concealed storage is slotted in under the stairs.

Case Study
Working from home, London

1 The "library" staircase connecting the first and second levels. High-level shelving is accessed by a ladder from the half-landing. The staircase was paneled in to create concealed storage.
2 The living room end of the main space on the lower floor features a built-in couch that runs the width of the room and a TV mounted on a bracket to keep the floor area clear.
3 The new entrance vestibule extends into what was a small cabinet to create more space with room for bike storage.
4 At the far end of the main living area is a long and narrow red dining table made of MDF. Low, semi-built-in benches house a collection of old vinyl; additional seating is provided by low stools.
5 The new bathroom features a wall-hung toilet. Storage is concealed behind tongue-and-groove matchboarding; a sheet of floor-to-ceiling mirror runs behind the sink.

LEVEL ONE

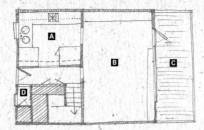

LEVEL TWO

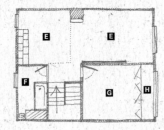

LOFT

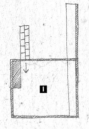

A Kitchen
B Living room
C Patio
D Hall storage
E Open-concept work space
F Bathroom
G Bedroom
H Built-in cupboards
I Loft level

The redesign of the interior provided an opportunity to to build in as much storage space as possible

5

space-saving "monk's stairs" (or "paddle steps"). A small back bedroom was converted into a bathroom, incorporating what had formerly been a separate toilet.

The redesign of the interior space provided an opportunity to build in as much storage as possible. Flush white-painted panels on push-catches are slotted in under stairs and in the hallway to keep possessions hidden from view, while the bathroom and bedroom also include concealed storage. The stairs connecting the first and second level became a "library," with high-level shelves accessed by a ladder from the half-landing.

Decorating and furnishing choices were designed to enhance the sense of space. Downstairs, the flooring is linoleum throughout; upstairs is carpeted. Walls are painted a soft stone color. Furniture is low – in the living area seating is provided by a built-in couch running the width of the room. Opposite is a simple long red table (made of MDF to the architect's design and gloss-painted), with seating provided by semi-fixed benches that double as storage spaces and stools. Even the TV is mounted on a bracket to keep the floor space free.

What One-bedroom split-level apartment with home office on the 31st and 32nd floors of a tower block.
Where Porte d'Italie, Paris.
Problem Poorly laid out apartment with small loft, dark balcony and dreary interior decoration.

Goal To increase floor area of loft to make room for home office and bedroom. To improve decoration.
Solution Repositioning the stairs to the loft level allowed for an extension of floor area to accommodate a home office and sleeping area

above. The kitchen was also increased in size. Complete redecoration all in white enhanced the sense of space and light.

1

White light

This split-level apartment, occupying the 31st and 32nd floors of the top of a tower block in Paris, faces east and every morning it is bathed in rosy dawn light. When the owner, a designer and stylist, bought the apartment it looked very different from the glowing light-filled space it is today. The flooring throughout was orange carpet; there was a great deal of exposed wood and the loft level was very cramped.

The major structural alteration, for which the owner engaged the services of an architect, was to reposition the stairs. The original staircase went up the side of the apartment, a layout that resulted in wasted space. The new central position of the stairs allowed for the extension of the loft to provide room for a home office on one side and a sleeping area on the other. At the same time, the new open metal staircase created a more dynamic layout on the lower floor, effectively distinguishing between the living area and the kitchen/dining area without any loss of light or views. The new layout also meant that a small storage area could be slotted in under the loft on one side, while the existing kitchen could be

2

Large metal-framed windows flood the interior with morning light; because the apartment is so high up, there was no need to worry about privacy

1 The view underneath the central open stairs. The original staircase was at the side of the apartment. The new metal stairs with their open treads and railings were painted all white to blend in unobtrusively with the rest of the space.
2 Looking across the L-shaped kitchen counter toward the living area. Simple canvas director's chairs preserve a lightness of touch. Large metal-framed windows let in the light.
3 The newly designed and enlarged kitchen is separated by a counter from the dining area. The counter contains cupboards and open shelving on both sides.

Case Study
White light,
Paris

The apartment was decorated in pure white – both to make the most of the light and views and to serve as a pristine backdrop for colorful displays

1

FIRST LEVEL   LOFT

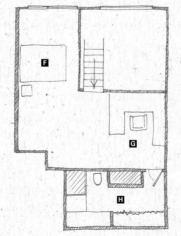

A Balcony	**E** Cloakroom
B Dining area	**F** Bedroom area
C Living area	**G** Work space
D Kitchen	**H** Bathroom

2

1 The floor of the balcony was painted white to allow the outside space to read as an extension of the interior. The simple garden furniture is also white.

2 The home office on the loft level, where the owner comes up with schemes for window displays, photo shoots and corporate parties. White box folders on open shelves recede into the background, while colorful decorative objects take pride of place.

3 At the other end of the enlarged loft is a sleeping area. The open railings of the balustrade interrupt light and views only minimally. A white shelf unit at the end of the bed provides more space for decorative display.

3

enlarged on the other. A new L-shaped counter now defines the kitchen area, with shelves and cupboards on each side of the shorter arm of the L.

Large metal-framed windows flood the interior with morning light. Because the apartment is so high up, there was no need to worry about privacy or overlooking, but external roller blinds allow light control when the sun is very strong.

The apartment was decorated in pure white – both to make the most of the light and views and to serve as a pristine backdrop for colorful displays. The floor is white vinyl. The external balcony was also painted white to extend the interior space visually. Walls, stairs, light fixtures and much of the furniture are also plain white. This allows the owner, who enjoys "playing with little objects," to vary the look of the apartment with color and displays. Sometimes displays are coordinated – all red, for example, at Christmas. With the basic shell and most of the furnishings white, and no dominant pictures on the wall or rugs underfoot, the apartment becomes a showcase in which the owner can express her delight in all the colors of the rainbow.

Case Study
One-bedroom apartment, New York

What One-bedroom apartment in a co-op building.
Where New York.
Problem Originally an uninspiring bachelor with a flimsy dividing wall badly positioned so as to interrupt the picture window and heating/air conditioning unit.

Goal To make a better use of the very limited space – 520 sq. ft. (48 m²) – while maximizing storage space for possessions and equipment. To make the most of the spectacular view across Chelsea to downtown Manhattan.

Solution The concept was to treat the apartment as a mini loft, opening out the spaces as much as possible to improve light and views. The design of built-in storage dictated the architectural approach, with the nexus of the plan being the teak room divider that separates the living area from the bedroom. A limited palette of high-quality finishes provides visual unity. Every square inch of storage space was planned according to the client's needs to provide a seamless practicality of use.

1

The basic concept behind the redesign of this space was to treat the apartment as a mini loft while providing a degree of separation between public and private space

A place for everything

Located in an unprepossessing postwar white brick co-op building of the sort that are ubiquitous in New York, this one-bedroom apartment had little to recommend it on first sight, except for its clear and unobstructed view across Chelsea to downtown Manhattan. The apartment had previously been used as a studio and had been poorly converted. The thin, flimsy partition that had been flung up to divide the bedroom from the living room was oddly positioned, in such a way as to interrupt the long south-facing picture window – as well as the heating/air conditioning unit.

The basic concept behind the redesign of this space was to treat the apartment as a mini loft while providing a degree of separation between public and private space. With the apartment measuring only 520 sq. ft. (48 m²), the challenge was to provide sufficient concealed storage to house necessary domestic equipment and possessions, which in turn meant planning the storage so that it was tailor-made for the client. As a consequence, storage space dictated the overall architectural approach.

1 The main living area, with its panoramic view of Manhattan. The teak divider, which screens the bedroom, has foldaway doors, so that it is possible to operate and watch the TV from both the living room and bedroom side.
2 The redesigned kitchen extends into a former broom closet and is fitted out with ash and stainless steel cupboards. Undercounter appliances are space-saving.
3 A compact home office has been neatly integrated into the original coat closet in the foyer.

Case Study
A place for everything, New York

The challenge was to provide sufficient concealed storage to house domestic equipment and possessions, so all storage had to be tailor-made for the client

1 The shower room is minimally separated from the sleeping area by floor-to-ceiling panels of clear glass hung with curtains. When the curtains are open, the view over the city can be enjoyed from the shower. The shower room is clad in brick-shaped tiles of Carrara marble; taps and hardware are stainless steel, while the fixtures are white porcelain.

2 An acid-etched glass panel that slides into the teak divider separates the bedroom/shower room from the living area. New oak flooring stained chocolate brown provides visual unity. The bed is raised up on a low platform made of ash that extends beyond each side of the mattress to form a shelf.

3 White lacquer panels and doors conceal custom-made storage. The storage units extend along the north wall of the living room into the shower room. On the opposite side, low windowsill cabinets enhance the sense of space while providing more room for storing everyday belongings and possessions.

A Kitchen
B Concealed desk
C Entrance hall
D Storage
E Open-concept living room
F Room divider/storage
G Shower room
H Bedroom

The original layout featured a long, wide entrance foyer extending from the living room. This was reconfigured as a square volume using white-lacquered panel doors. The resulting narrower passage through to the new living space allowed for deep closets, and the former coat closet became a home office. The kitchen, adjacent to the foyer, was extended into a former broom closet and refitted with ash and stainless steel cabinets and undercounter appliances.

Once the partition wall was removed, the living room, bedroom and shower room could be conceived as a single space. The large south-facing picture window lights the living room and bedroom, and provides spatial continuity. An element of separation and privacy is provided by the new teak room divider that houses storage and electronic equipment. This is underlit, so that it appears to float over the floor.

A new oak floor, stained dark chocolate, creates a continuous plane of color through the entire space. The ceiling is another continuous plane, floating over the room divider and washed by uplighting. Another unifying aspect to the design is the white lacquer doors and panels of concealed storage, which start in the foyer, wrap around the north wall of the living room and continue into the shower room. Storage has been designed in such a careful custom-made way that the client can leave the shower, access the contents of various closets to dress and walk to the door, collecting cellphone and keys from a custom-designed floating ash box in the foyer. A place for everything and everything in its place.

Case Study
Family house, London

What Three-bedroom house on ground and basement levels, with rooftop addition.
Where Hampstead, London.
Problem The original property, built in the 1960s on 19th-century foundations, was dark and poorly planned, with 70 percent of the accommodation underground. This former home of modernist painter Ben Nicholson was surrounded by listed 18th- and 19th-century properties in an historic area.
Goal To replace the ground-floor level with a new house within the original footprint and height. To draw as much light as possible down into the basement. To add an office within a second-story addition.
Solution Substantial excavation created a series of lightwells and a courtyard to brighten up basement rooms. Windows were taken up beyond ceiling height, where possible, to improve light angles. Materials were used to add warmth to natural light. A new hallway at basement level became the organizing element for what had been a warren of rooms. Roofs were pitched steeply to avoid overshadowing neighboring properties.

1

2

3

1 The front elevation of the house, showing the second-story office addition. On the other side of the front wall is the front courtyard, which is inset with glass panels that draw light down into lightwells.
2 In the entrance hall a suspended closet stops short of the floor and ceiling to enhance the sense of space. To the right is a corner of a lightwell that descends to the basement level.
3 The main ground-floor space is an open-concept kitchen/dining room/living room. A margin of lowered ceiling running around the perimeter of the room serves as a framing device. The kitchen units and island are made of black granite and anthracite self-colored MDF to give them a sculptural quality, so their functional purpose is less obtrusive.
4 Straight-grain Douglas fir flooring is laid across the width of the room, leading the eye out to the front courtyard.

Drawing down the light

It may have once been the home of British painter Ben Nicholson, but heritage and conservation bodies could find little about the property worth conserving. Neither were neighbors sorry to see the "bungalow," with its ugly black plastic roof, go. That was good news for the new owners of the house, both architects, whose plans were to demolish the existing structure down to ground level and start again.

The challenge was to create a light-filled home working within the parameters of the building's original footprint and height – no easy task, since 70 percent of the property was at basement level. The chief strategy involved substantial excavation to create a series of lightwells at the front of the property and a new courtyard at the back to draw natural light down into the gloomy basement rooms.

The original house was poorly planned, with bedrooms on the ground floor and living areas in the basement. This planning was reversed and most of the new ground floor is now an open-concept area with a kitchen at one end, a living area at the other and a dining area in the center. Sheets of glass connect

1 A corner of a lightwell at basement level. Running the windows above ceiling height maximizes the amount of natural light by increasing the "sky factor."
2 A view of the back courtyard, paved in York stone, from one of the children's bedrooms. The windows are framed in Douglas fir, which softens and warms the quality of light. The external space is viewed as an extension of the interior.
3 A view through to the children's playroom, showing a corner of a lightwell. In addition to bringing light down below ground, the lightwells also help prevent water penetration. Few of the walls in the basement rooms are earth-retaining. Instead, the external faces of the lightwells serve as second skins to stop water ingress.
4 The basement hallway provides a long vista and an important organizing element. The Douglas fir flooring is laid to lead the eye down the hall.

the space to the front courtyard. Various framing devices, accentuated by lighting, help define the large open-concept ground floor. At basement level a new hallway running the width of the building and facing into the lightwells has become the chief organizing element that connects the previously dark rooms.

Throughout the house, windows are extended as far as they will go. Wherever possible, they are pushed above ceiling height to improve the light angles. The degree of daylight a room receives is determined by the "sky factor" – in other words, how much of the sky (the light source) is visible. By pushing the glass upward by only 4 in. (10 cm) or so, the sky factor can be doubled. Big sheets of glass also allow external spaces to be seen as extensions of internal rooms.

Material choices also work to enhance the quality of light. Flooring and internal window frames are warm-toned Douglas fir, which makes gray skies seem bluer. Courtyard paving is in York stone, sourced from a quarry that produces stone of a warmer color than the standard gray shades. Along with concrete plinths, plaster, curtains and wallpapered planes, the effect is to create a subtle palette of textures and tones.

As the master bedroom is entered through the master bathroom, treating the sink and tub as sculptural elements is less discordant. The bathtub is enclosed in concrete and the sink is set on a concrete plinth. **5** The front courtyard showing panels of glass above the lightwells.

3

4

Substantial excavation created a series of lightwells at the front of the property and a new courtyard at the back to draw light down into the gloomy basement rooms

5

GROUND FLOOR

BASEMENT

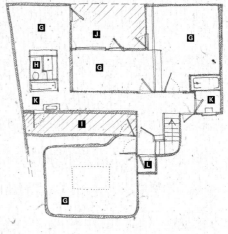

SECOND STORY

A Office	**G** Bedroom
B Nook/snug	**H** Shower
C Main living area	**I** Lightwell
D Kitchen area	**J** Back courtyard
E Void	**K** Bathroom
F Front courtyard	**L** Toilet

What Narrow, single-story family house.
Where Adachi-ward, Tokyo
Problem Newly built house for a young family on a very restricted narrow site. The site is in an area where population density is very high and few houses have any outdoor space. The challenge was to create an interior that was as light, open and airy as possible, and that made the most of any connection with outdoor areas.
Solution The concept was a modern reinterpretation of the traditional Japanese engawa, or porch. The shape of the site dictated a long, narrow plan, with the living space arranged in a linear fashion along the length of the building. The wall of the house that faces the inner courtyard is 52 ft. (16 m) of glass sliding doors, which open completely, effectively turning the house itself into a porch. With the wife's mother, father, brother and sister-in-law living in the house across the courtyard, and the building to the rear housing the family business, the new building turns the area into a private compound.

Bringing the outside in

The Engawa House was designed to accommodate a young family. When land came up for sale next to the house where the wife's parents, brother and sister-in-law lived, she and her husband decided to buy the site and commission a newly built home for themselves. A building that houses the family construction business is nearby. The new house effectively creates a private inner courtyard or family compound.

Space is at a premium in Japan and this location is no exception; most houses in the vicinity take up their entire sites, with no yards. Before the Engawa House was built, the porch of the grandparents' house faced a massive wall only 20 in. (50 cm) distant. Rather than infill the site, the architects decided to arrange a single-story house along the southern side boundary bordering the road. This left enough space between it and the grandparents' house to create a yard. As the new house was only one story high, the yard would not be overshadowed.

On the southern side of the house, the flanking wall rises to a height of 7 ft. (2.2 m), with a long horizontal opening, or clerestory, at a high level to

1 The wood-framed and wood-clad house, showing the extensive 52 ft. (16 m) opening on the north side.
2 The functional bathroom cubicle is partitioned from the children's room to the left and the master bedroom to the right by solid wood walls

6½ ft. (2 m) high. Above is the roof void and the high-level south-facing windows.
3 The house viewed from the inner courtyard, showing the linear layout: open-concept kitchen, dining and living area; children's room, bathroom and master bedroom.

4 The kitchen is arranged along the length of an island counter with a metal-clad upstand screening kitchen activity. The high-level openings create a natural air flow that cools the interior in summer.

3

4

The difference in height between the south-facing and north-facing openings gives the building an unusual appearance, as if it were a set of parallel bars

1 The entire south wall of the house is equipped with storage cupboards to house all the family's possessions. Box-like partitions separate the more private areas.

2 Exterior view of the opened-up house from the courtyard. Heating is supplied by a closed stove.

3 The main entrance on the street, or south-facing, frontage.

preserve privacy while giving views of the sky. The northern, or inner, wall, by contrast, is entirely open. Nine floor-to-ceiling glass doors slide back to create a 52 ft. (16 m) opening that effectively transforms the house into a porch in good weather. The result is a simple rectangular box 53 ft. (16.2 m) long by 15 ft. (4.6 m) wide, enclosed by two L-shaped frames.

The main construction material is wood, chosen for its unifying quality. The vast open wall meant that additional reinforcement had to be provided to accommodate any movement in the lumber. The difference in height between the south-facing and north-facing openings gives the building an unusual appearance, as if it were a set of uneven parallel bars.

Internally, the space is conceived as a single volume. The roof is 11½ ft. (3.5 m) high; internal partitions extend only to 6½ ft. (2 m), which allows for natural ventilation and promotes internal climate control. Steam rising from the bathroom cubicle dissipates within the roof space. Similarly, kitchen fumes rise up to the lofty roof level and are evacuated by an industrial exhaust fan. In the summer, warm air rises toward the roof and is drawn out of the high windows.

Nine floor-to-ceiling glass doors slide back to create a 52 ft. (16 m) opening that effectively transforms the house into a porch in good weather

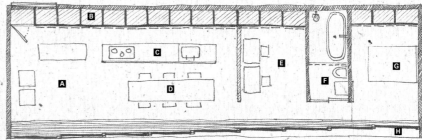

A Living area
B Built-in storage
C Kitchen area
D Dining area
E Children's area
F Bathroom
G Master bedroom
H Sliding doors

Suppliers

Advice

American Institute of Architects (AIA)
1735 New York Ave NW
Washington, DC 20006
202.626.7300
800.242.3837
www.aia.org

American Society of Interior Designers (ASID)
608 Massachusetts Ave NE
Washington, DC 20002
202.546.3480
www.asid.org

BuilderDirectory.com
www.builderdirectory.com
Offers a state-by-state online search guide to locate architects, builders, engineers and other key professionals.

cDecor.com
310.276.5001
www.cdecor.com
Online magazine that features directories of interior designers, sources and showrooms.

Canadian Architecture
www.canadianarchitecture.com
Lists architects, engineers, contractors, building materials, manufacturers and suppliers in Canada.

The Council of Better Business Bureaus (BBB)
4200 Wilson Blvd, Suite 800
Arlington, VA
703.276.0100

and

The Canadian Council of Better Business Bureaus
2 St. Clair Ave E
Toronto, ON M4T 2T5
www.bbb.org
This website provides valuable information on planning and financing your project, hiring a contractor, getting a building permit, and contract negotiations and locating your nearest BBB.

Home Improvement Lenders Association
1625 Massachusetts Ave NW, Suite 601
Washington, DC 20036
202.939.1770
Useful information on planning, financing and executing home improvement projects.

Interior Designers Canada
717 Church Street
Toronto, ON M4W 2M5
416.594.9310
www.interiordesigncanada.org
Provides links to provincial association members with resource directories.

National Association of Home Builders
1201 15th Street NW
Washington, DC 20005
202.266.8200
800.368.5242
www.nahb.org

National Association of the Remodeling Industry (NARI)
www.nari.org
Resource for contractors and suppliers, tips and homeowner's guide.

Royal Architectural Institute of Canada
330-55 Murray Street
Ottawa, ON K1N 5M3
613.241.3600
www.raic.org

General Home Furnishings & One-Stop Shops

Anthropologie
www.anthropologie.com
Large selection of home decor items. only store locator for U.S. and online shopping for U.S. and Canada.

Blu Dot
3306 Fifth Street NE
Minneapolis, MN 55418
www.bludot.com
Affordable contemporary designs for home furnishings. Only store locator for U.S. and Canada.

BoConcept
www.boconcept.com
Contemporary retail furniture chain from Denmark. Online store locator for U.S. and Canada.

Branch
1684 15th Street
San Francisco, CA 94103
415.341.1824
Sustainable design furniture and accessories. Online shopping in U.S.

Brookstone
800.846.3000
www.brookstone.com
This exclusive hardware specialty shop is known for its hard-to-find tools; also offers storage solutions for the home. Online store locator and shopping in U.S.

California Closets
1000 Fourth Street, Suite 800
San Rafael, CA 94901
415.256.8500
www.calclosets.com
Closets and storage solutions for bedrooms, home offices, garages, living rooms, kitchens and utility rooms. Consultation and design service. Website has showroom locator for U.S. and Canada.

CB2
3737 North Lincoln Ave
Chicago, Il 60613
800.606.6252
www.cb2.com
Offshoot of Crate and Barrel. Online shopping available in U.S. and Canada.

The Conran Shop
407 East 59th Street
New York, NY 10022
212.755.9097
www.conran.com
Contemporary furniture and interiors with online shopping available in U.S.

Contemporary Furniture
2525 Elmwood Ave
Buffalo, NY 14217
716.875.3237
800.477.2285
www.contemporaryfurniture.com
Online furniture site specializing in contemporary and Scandinavian designs.

Crate & Barrel
800.967.6696
www.crateandbarrel.com
Furniture and kitchen accessories. Online store locator and shopping in U.S.

De La Espada
www.delaespada.com
Solid lumber furniture with a modernist esthetic. Showrooms in New York and San Francisco, online shopping in U.S. and Canada.

Design Within Reach
415.248.5397
800.944.2233
www.dwr.com
Affordable modern furniture designs. Studios across the U.S., online shopping in the U.S. and Canada.

EasyClosets
908.647.6020
800.910.0129
www.easyclosets.com
Storage solutions for chests, pantries and laundry rooms.

Furniture.com
www.furniture.com
Online store featuring an array of furniture as well as a design-advice section.

FurnitureFind
800.362.7632
www.furniturefind.com
Online shopping with a huge selection of furniture in all categories, with resources section, information and tips.

GE Lighting
www.gelighting.com
Take a tour through the GE Virtual House to compare alternative lighting solutions.

Hammacher Schlemmer
147 East 57th Street
New York, NY 10022
800.321.1484
www.hammacher.com
Specialty store with online shopping available in U.S. and Canada.

Home Depot
www.homedepot.com
www.homedepot.ca
Huge selection of home products online. Stores throughout U.S. and Canada.

Home Focus Catalog
800.221.6771
www.homefocuscatalog.com
Extensive selection of storage items for indoors and outdoors. Shop online or call for a catalog.

Hudson House
1619 Walnut Street
Kansas City, MO 64108
816.412.3629
www.hudsonhomeonline.com
Modern furniture and accessories from midwest designers.

IKEA
800.434.4532 (U.S.)
866.866.4532 (Canada)
www.ikea.com
All kinds of furniture and fittings including kitchens and bathrooms. Online catalog and store locator.

Jennifer Convertibles
www.jenniferfurniture.com
Large discount retailer specializing in sofa beds. Online showroom locator in U.S.

The Magazine
1823 Eastshore Highway
Berkeley, CA 94710
510.549.2282
www.themagazine.info
Modern Furniture and accessories. Online shopping available in U.S. and Canada.

Organize.com
P.O. Box 2348
Riverside, CA 92516
800.600.9817
www.organize-everything.com
Organizers for closets and every room in the house; special kids' storage line. Online shopping in U.S.

Pier 1
800.245.4595
www.pier1.com
Storage furniture and accessories. Online store locator and shopping in U.S. and Canada.

Pottery Barn
888.779.5176
www.potterybarn.com
Storage furniture and accessories. Online locator for stores across the U.S. and Canada.

Pure Design
800.483.5643
www.puredesignonline.com
Collection of modern tables, chairs, shelving and accessories. Online shopping available in U.S. and Canada.

Rona
www.rona.ca
Huge selection of home products. Website has locator for over 600 retail stores and hardware outlets across Canada.

Room
182 Duane Street
New York, NY 10013
888.420.7666
www.roomonline.com
High-end modern design furniture.

Room & Board
800.301.9720
www.roomandboard.com
Wide selection of contemporary furniture and accessories. Online store locator for U.S. and online shopping in U.S. and Canada.

Stacks and Stacks
1045 Hensley Street
Richmond, CA 94801
800.761.5222
www.stacksandstacks.com
Shop online for closet organizers, shelving, bookcases, entertainment centers and desks. Available in U.S.

Target
800.591.3869
www.target.com
Popular chain for affordable furniture and furnishings. Online catalog and store locator for U.S.

The Terence Conran Shop
Bridgemarket, 407 East 59th Street
New York, NY 10022
212.755.9079
Contemporary storage furniture and accessories.

Suppliers

Umbra
800.387.5122
www.umbra.com
*Contemporary furniture
and accessories. Online
shopping and retail locator
in U.S. and Canada.*

Williams & Sonoma Home
888.922.4108
www.wshome.com
*Furniture and accessories.
Online store locator and
shopping in U.S.*

Kitchens

SEE ALSO UNDER
GENERAL HOME FURNISHINGS

Alno
617.482.2566
www.alno.com
*Contemporary kitchen
cabinetry. Online dealer
locator for U.S. and Canada.*

Boffi Studio
www.boffi.com
*Compact kitchen designs.
Online dealer locator for
U.S. and Canada.*

Bulthaup
800.808.2923
www.bulthaup.com
*High quality contemporary
fitted and unfitted kitchens.*

Downsview Kitchens
2635 Rena Road
Mississauga, ON L4T 1G6
(905) 677-9354
www.downsviewkitchens
.com
*Contemporary and classic
kitchen cabinetry. Online
showroom locator for U.S.
and Canada.*

ISS Designs
949.366.0780
877.477.5487
www.issdesigns.com
*Modern system shelving.
Online shopping available in
U.S.*

Johnny Grey
800.640.7879
www.johnnygrey.com
*Contemporary kitchen
manufacturer that will
provide design planning
services.*

The Kennebec Company
1 Front Street
Bath, ME 04530
207.443.2131
www.kennebeccompany.com
*Handcrafted wooden
cabinetry.*

Poggenpohl
www.poggenpohl.de
*Contemporary kitchens.
Online showroom and
dealer locator for U.S. and
Canada.*

Siematic
www.siematic.com
*Contemporary kitchen
designs available
worldwide.*

Smallbone
135 East 65th Street
New York, NY 10021
212.288.3454
www.smallbone.co.uk
Classic kitchen designs.

Bathrooms

SEE ALSO UNDER
GENERAL HOME FURNISHINGS

Agape
www.agapedesign.it
*Bathroom products and
accessories. Online dealer
locator for U.S. and Canada.*

American-Standard
800.821.7700
www.americanstandard
-us.com
*Kitchen and bath fixtures.
Online store locator for U.S.*

Ann Sacks
503.243.3281
800.278.8453
www.annsacks.com
*Wide range of fine tile,
stone and plumbing
products. Online store and
dealer locator for U.S. and
Canada.*

Bed Bath and Beyond
800.462.3966
www.bedbathandbeyond.com
*only store locator for U.S.
only.*

Designer Plumbing
866.232.8238
www.designerplumbing.com
*Wide selections of
bathroom fixtures and
accessories. Online
shopping in U.S. and
Canada.*

Dornbracht
www.dornbracht.com
*Contemporary designs for
the bathroom and kitchen
Online retailer locator for
U.S. and Canada.*

Duravit USA, Inc
1750 Breckinridge Parkway,
Suite 500
Duluth, GA 30096
770.931.3575
888.387.2848
www.duravit.us
Online retailer locator for U.S.

Ginger's
95 Ronald Ave
Toronto, ON M6B 4L9
416.787.1787
888.444.3292
*High-end bath and kitchen
features.*

Herbeau
239.417.5368
www.herbeau.com
*Manufacturer of authentic
19th century kitchen and
bath fixtures. Online dealer
locator for U.S. and Canada.*

Kohler Co.
800.456.4537
www.kohler.com
Kitchen and bath fixtures.
Online dealer locator in U.S.
and Canada.

Sherle Wagner
International
60 East 57th Street
New York, NY 10022
212.758.3300
www.sherlewagner.com
Exclusive bathroom fixtures
and hardware. Online
showroom locator for U.S.

Urban Archaeology
212.431.4646
www.urbanarchaeology
.com
Lighting, bathroom fixtures
and accessories. Online
dealer locator for U.S only.

Villeroy & Boch
www.villeroy-boch.com
Manufacturers of bathroom
products and other lifestyle
products. Online showroom
locator.

Vintage Tub and Bath
877.868.1369
www.vintagetub.com
Manufacturer of bathroom
fixtures specializing in claw
foot tubs. Online shopping
in U.S. and Canada.

Waterworks
800.899.6757
www.waterworks.com
Manufactures of kitchen
and bathroom products.
Online dealer locator for
U.S. and Canada.

Bedrooms
SEE ALSO UNDER
GENERAL HOME FURNISHINGS

Cath Kidston
212.343.0223
www.cathkidston.com
Retro accessories, kitchen
containers and stationery.
Online catalog and retail
outlets in New York and Los
Angeles.

Closet Valet
2033 Concourse Drive
St Louis, MO 63146
866.381.5465
314.447.0300
www.closetvalet.com
Shop online for specialty
closet organizers and
accessories, including built-
in ironing boards, valet
closet rods, belt racks and
tie racks.

Flying Beds
5125 E. Stapleton Drive
   North
Denver, CO 80216
303.333.3052
888.892.4645
www.flyingbeds.com
Unique selection of wall
beds. Online shopping
available in U.S.

Home Offices &
Work Areas
SEE ALSO UNDER
GENERAL HOME FURNISHINGS

Brookstone
800.846.3000
www.brookstone.com
Exclusive hardware
specialty shop, selling
storage solutions for
closets, kitchens, home
offices and garages. Online
catalog and store locator in
U.S.

elfa
www2.elfa.com
Great selection of modern
storage products and
shelving units. Online dealer
locator for U.S. and Canada.

Gardeners Edge
888.556.5676
www.gardenersedge.com
Outdoor furniture and
garden accents. Online
shopping in U.S.

HomeOfficeDirect.com
8870 Darrow Road,
   Suite F106, Box 222
Twinsburg, OH 44087
877.709.9700
www.homeofficedirect.com
Ready to assemble office
furniture. Online shopping in
U.S.

Knoll International
800.343.5665
www.knoll.com
High quality home office
furniture. Online locator of
showrooms and dealers in
U.S. and Canada.

Lee Valley Tools
800.267.8735 (U.S.)
800.267.8761 (Canada)
www.leevalley.com
Large selection of gardening
tools and accessories.
Online store locator and
online shopping in U.S. and
Canada.

Paperchase
www.paperchase.co.uk
Design-led stationery.
Products are sold in Borders
stores across the U.S.

Turnstone
www.turnstonefurniture.com
Contemporary office
furniture. Online dealer
locator for U.S. and Canada.

Workbench
www.workbenchfurniture
.com
Links to websites selling
furniture and storage for
home offices.

Index

Index

Credits

Architects featured in the case studies

■ PAGES 190–193

Dry Design
5727 Venice Boulevard
Los Angeles
CA 90019
T + 1 323 954 9084
F + 1 323 954 9085

www.drydesign.com

■ PAGES 202 – 205

Messana O'Rorke
118 West 22nd Street
Ninth Floor
New York
NY 10011
T + 1 212 807 1960
F + 1 212 807 1966

www.messanaororke.com

■ PAGES 206 – 209

Woollacott Gilmartin Architects
2b Pilgrims Lane
London
NW3.1SL
T + 44 20 7431 9983

■ PAGES 210 – 213

Tezuka Architects
1-19-9-3F Todoroki Setagaya
Tokyo 158-0082
Japan
T + 81 3 3703 7056
F + 81 3 3703 7038

www.tezuka-arch.com

The publisher would like to thank the following photographers, agencies and architects for their kind permission to reproduce the following photographs:

6–7 Sacha Kletzsch (Architects: Richard Horden, Horden Cherry Lee, London, Haack Hopfner, Munich); 8 Edmund Sumner /View (Architect: Atelier Bow-Wow); 9 Jake Fitzjones/Living Etc/IPC Syndication; 10 above Courtesy of Hotel Puerta America (Photographer: Rafael Vargas, Designer: Richard Gluckman); 10 below Courtesy of Hotel Puerta America (Photographer: Rafael Vargas, Designer: Ron Arad); 12 Vercruysse and Dujardin (Architect: Genevieve Marginet); 12 above left Courtesy of Hotel Puerta America (Photographer: Rafael Vargas, Designer: Ron Arad); 12 above right Courtesy of Hotel Puerta America (Photographer: Rafael Vargas, Designer: Mariscal & Salas); 12 below Courtesy of Hotel Puerta America (Photographer: Rafael Vargas, Designer: Zaha Hadid); 13 Bert Leandersson (Design: Optibo & White Design); 14 above Courtesy of Hanse Haus GmbH; 14 below Stellan Herner; 15 above Dre Wapenaar 1998 (Photographer: Robbert R. Roos); 15 below Ralph Richter /Architekturphoto/Arcaid (Mart de Jong/Architectenbureau De Vijf); 18–19 Bénédicte Ausset/Marie Claire Maison (Designer: Francois Pascal, Architects Aude Pichard & Pascal Rodgriquez); 20–21 Bieke Claessens /Photozest (Designer: Jan De Vis); 21 Luke White/The Interior Archive; 22 Jan Baldwin /Narratives (Architects: MMM Architects); 26 above Chris Tubbs/Conran Octopus (Woollacott Gilmartin Architects); 26 below left Bénédicte Ausset/Marie Claire Maison (Stylist: Gaël Reyre); 26 below

right Paul Lepreux/Marie Claire Maison (Inspired by Le Corbusier); 26-27 Verne Fotografie; 28 Jefferson Smith/Media10 Syndication (Architect: van Heyningen & Haward); 29 above Kennet Havgaard/House of Pictures; 29 below Johnny Bouchier/Red Cover (Designer: John Haworth); 30-31 Simon Upton/The Interior Archive (Architect: Julian Powell-Tuck); 32 Hotze Eisma/Sanoma Uitgevers (Stylist: Marianne Lunning); 33 Sue Barr/View (Architect: Robert Dye); 34 Mark Luscombe-Whyte/The Interior Archive (Owner: Plum); 34–35 Chris Tubbs/Conran Octopus (Woollacott Gilmartin Architects); 35 Sturla Bakken; 36 Jan Baldwin/Narratives (Architects: Kay Hartmann Architects); 36 above Julian Cornish-Trestrail/Roland Cowan Architects; 36 below Ferran Freixa/RBA; 38 Ray Main /Mainstream Images; 38-39 Ray Main/Mainstream Images (Architect: Gregory Philips); 39 Eugeni Pons/RBA; 40–41 Xavier Béjot/Tripod (Architect: Sean McEvoy); 42 above Paul Massey/Living Etc/IPC Syndication; 42 below Edmund Sumner/View (Architect: Theme 2 Architects); 42–43 Edmund Sumner/View (Architect: Jun Aoki); 46 Henry Wilson/Red Cover (Architects: Ian Chee and Von Yee Wong); 47 above left Paul Ryan /International Interiors (Designer: Mathias Wagmo); 47 above right Jan Baldwin/Narratives (Architect: Annalie Riches); 47 below Paul Massey/Living Etc/IPC Syndication; 48 Dexter Hodges/Medita (Design: Fernando Salas); 48–49 Ray Main/Mainstream Images; 49 Jason Lowe; 50 above Jan Baldwin/Narratives (Architect: Kay Hartmann Architects); 50 below Andreas von Einsiedel (Architect: Sarah Featherstone); 50–51 Paul Ryan/International

Interiors; 51 Ray Main /Mainstream Images (Juerkearchitekten); 54–55 Ake E:son Lindman; 56 Jan Baldwin /Narratives (Architect: Jonathan Clark); 56–57 Ray Main /Mainstream Images (Echodesign);57 Richard Powers (Designer: Karim Rashid); 58–59 Giulio Oriani/Vega MG; 59 Amparo Garrido/RBA; 60 Bruno Helbling/Zapaimages (Architect: Gus Wuesteman); 61 Ake E:son Lindman; 62 Jason Lowe/Red Cover; 62–63 Courtesy of Stephen Varady Architecture; 63 Giulio Oriani/Vega MG; 64 left Courtesy of Hotel Puerta America (Photographer: Rafael Vargas, Designers: Victorio - Lucchino); 64 right Gianni Basso/Vega MG; 65 Ray Main /Mainstream Images; 65 right Bert Leandersson (Design: Optibo & White Design); 66–67 Vercruysse and Dujardin (Designer: Dirk Meylaerts); 68 above Jan Baldwin/Narratives (Architect: Annalie Riches); 68 below Reto Guntli /Zapaimages (Architect: Kenichi Yokohori); 69 above Ed Reeve/Red Cover (Architect: William Tozer); 69 below Bruno Helbling/Zapaimages (Architect: Gus Wuestemann); 70–71 Henry Wilson/Red Cover (Architects: Ian Chee and Voon Yee Wong); 71 Alexander van Berge/Taverne Agency (Architect: Jen Alkema); 72 left Eugeni Pons/Arcaid (Architect: Anne Bugugnani); 73 left Happyliving.dk/House of Pictures; 73 right Ken Hayden /Red Cover (Architect: John Pawson); 75 Grant Govier/Red Cover; 76–77 Brian Leonard /Narratives (Architect: Terry Dorrough Architects); 77 above Ray Main/Mainstream Images (Architect: Sergison Bates Architects); 77 below Ed Reeve/Red Cover; 78–79 Earl Carter/Taverne Agency (Stylist: Annemarie Kiely); 79 The Conran Shop; 80 left Alberto Piovano /Arcaid (Architect:Marco

Romanelli); 80 right James Balston/Media10 Syndication (Architect: Rob Gregory); 81 above left Thomas Ibsen (Design: Optibo & White Design); 81 above right Chris Tubbs/Red Cover; 81 below left James Balston/Media10 Syndication (Architect: Rob Gregory); 81 below right Paul Kelley; 82 above Elizabeth Felicella (Architect: Steven Learner Studio); 82 below left Ray Main /Mainstream Images (Architect: Littman Goddard Hogarth); 82 below right Ray Main /Mainstream Images (Architect: Littman Goddard Hogarth); 83 above left Elizabeth Felicella (Architect: Steven Learner Studio); 83 below Giulio Oriani/Vega MG; 84 Daniela Mac Adden/Sur Press Agencia (Stylist: Mariana Rapoport Architect: Martin Gomez); 85 Mel Yates; 86-87 Chris Tubbs/Conran Octopus (Architect: Adam Richards); 87 Eric Flogny/Marie Claire Maison (Stylist: Gael Reyre); 90–91 Edmund Sumner/View (Architect: Atelier Bow-Wow); 92–93 George Fetting (Architect & interior designer: Scott Weston); 96–97 Solvi dos Santos /Photozest; 98 E. Saillet /Photozest (Architect: Nesso Agency); 99 Paul Smoothy (Architect: 5th Studio Ltd); 100–101 Luke White/The Interior Archive (Designer: Neisha Crosland); 101 Kristian Septimius Krogh/House of Pictures; 102 left James Silverman/Red Cover; 102–103 Jean Luc Laloux (Architect: Bataille & Ibens); 103 above Solvi Dos Santos; 103 below Nicholas Kane/Arcaid (Architect: Theis & Khan); 104–105 Mark Luscombe Whyte/The Interior Archive (Designer: Francois Champsaur); 106 Ray Main/Mainstream Images (Arch Thorp); 107 Courtesy of Paul Archer Design Ltd.; 108 Richard Bryant/Arcaid (Architect: Seth

Stein); 109 Eugeni Pons/Arcaid (Architect: Anne Bugugnani); 110 Nigel Rigden (Architect: Henning Stummel); 112 left Sue Barr/View (Architect: Robert Dye); 112–113 above Matt Chisnall/Hut Architecture; 112–113 below Xavier Béjot /Tripod (Architect: Christian Baquiast); 113 Courtesy of GlasSpace; 114–115 Mark Luscombe Whyte/The Interior Archive (Architect: David Spence); 115 above John Maclean/View (Architect: Simon Leslie); 115 below Richard Waite (Architect: Paul Archer Design Ltd.); 116 David Churchill/Arcaid (Architect: De Metz Architects); 116–117 Dennis Gilbert/View (Architect: Peter Bernamont); 117 Paul Smoothy (Architect: Paul Archer Design & Fluid Structural); 120 above Matthew Antrobus/National Trust Photo Library; 120 below Chris Tubbs/Media10 Syndication (Architect: Sarah Wigglesworth); 121 Jacqueline Schellingerhout (Architect: Krill Architects); 122–123 Kilian O'Sullivan (Architect: Ullmayer Sylvester Architects); 123 above Nathalie Krag/Taverne Agency (Stylist: Gudrun Holck); 123 below Paul Smoothy (Architect: Sarah Wigglesworth); 126–127 Henry Wilson/Red Cover (Designer: Maria Speake); 128 above Eugeni Pons/Vega MG; 128 below Eugeni Pons/Vega MG; 129 above J. Hall/Photozest (Architect: Page Goolrick/Studio 40 M2); 129 below Graham Atkins-Hughes/Red Cover; 130–131 Ferran Freixa/RBA; 131 above Gaelle le Boulicaut (Architect: Nathalie Wolberg); 131 below Earl Carter/Taverne Agency (Stylist: Jean Wright); 132–133 Mark Luscombe-Whyte/The Interior Archive (Designer: Carden Cunietti); 134 Chris Tubbs/Conran Octopus (Architect: Adam Richards); 134–135 Chris Tubbs/Conran Octopus (Woollacott Gilmartin

Architects); 135 Bieke Claessens /Photozest; 136 above Dominic Blackmore; 136 below Kristian Septimius Krogh/House of Pictures; 137 above Jan Baldwin /Narratives (Architect: Jonathan Clark); 137 below Alan Weinitraub/Arcaid (Architect: Daniel Piechota); 138–139 Edmund Sumner/View (Architect: Endo Shuhei); 140–141 Jan Baldwin/Narratives (Penthouse Ziggurat Building, London); 142 left Jose Luis Hausmann/RBA; 142 right D. Vorillon/Photozest; 142–143 Magnus Anesund; 143 Courtesy of Boffi ('Single kitchen by Alberto Colonello); 144 above Ed Reeve/Red Cover; 144 below Winfried Heinze/Red Cover (Architect: Studio Azzuro); 144–145 Bieke Claessens (Architect: Lens Ass); 145 Ken Hayden/Red Cover; 146–148 left Ray Main /Mainstream Images; 148–149 Jose Luis Hausmann /RBA (Architects: E. Mosciaro & S. Contreras); 149 Gregory Goode/Marie Claire Maison (Sylist: Christiane Rivaux, Designer: Eric Goode); 150 Chris Tubbs/Conran Octopus (Architect: Adam Richards); 151 Dexter Hodges/Medita (Design: Alberto Guida, Architect: Roberto Provana); 152 Louis Lemaire/Sanoma Uitgevers (Stylist: Cleo Scheulderman); 152–153 Morley von Sternberg (Designer: Ab Rogers); 154 above Nathalie Krag/Taverne Agency (Stylist: Tami Christiansen); 154 below Sturla Bakken; 154 below left Jan Baldwin/Narratives (Architect: Kay Hartmann Architects); 155 left Hotze Eisma/Taverne Agency (Stylist: Reini Smit); 155 right Pia Ulin; 156–157 Mai-Linh/Marie Claire Maison (Stylist: Catherine Ardouin); 158–159 Edina van der Wyck/The Interior Archive (Designer: Geoff Powell); 159 Henry Wilson/Red Cover (David Mikhail);

160 above Ed Reeve/Red Cover (Architect: William Tozer); 160 below Grant Govier/Red Cover; 161 above Nathalie Krag/Taverne Agency (Stylist: Gudrun Holck); 161 below James Mitchell/Red Cover; 162 above left Dexter Hodges/Medita (Design: Fernando Salas); 162 above right Graham Atkins-Hughes/Red Cover; 162 below Luke White/The Interior Archive (Architect: Alex Monroe & Dan Brill); 163 above Simone de Geus/Sanoma Uitgevers; 163 below Luuk Geertsen /Sanoma Uitgevers; 164–165 Gaelle le Boulicaut (Architect: Nathalie Wolberg); 166 left Tim Evan Cook/Red Cover (Architect: Gunmar Orefelt); 166 right Chris Tubbs/Conran Octopus; 167 left Paul Lepreux/Marie Claire Maison (Designer Gilles Oudin); 167 right Dennis Brandsma /Sanoma Uitgevers; 168–169 Andrew Lawson (Designer: Nicola Rowe); 170 Alexis Armanet/Marie Claire Maison (Designer: Marie-Hélène De Taillac); 170-171 Marianne Majerus (Designer: Alastair Howe Architects); 172 Verity Welstead/Red Cover (Architect: Michael Gold); 172–173 above Maayke de Ridder (Designer: Ariane Prowato); 172–173 below Jerry Harpur/Harpur Garden Library (Designer: Fergus Garret); 173 Marianne Majerus (Designer: Marie Clarke); 174 Jerry Harpur/Gap Photos (Owners: Irena Sawyer & John Bishop); 174–175 Yann Monel/Marie Claire Maison (Stylist: Sylvia Marius); 175 Jerry Harpur/Harpur Garden Library (Designer: Declan Buckley); 176 Mark Luscombe-Whyte/The Interior Archive (Designer: Sarah Featherstone); 176–177 Mark York/Red Cover; 177 Henry Wilson/Red Cover (Architect: Voon Yee Wong, Interior Designer: Florence Lim); 178 above Marianne Majerus (Designer: David Matzdorf); 178 below Nicola Browne

(Designer: Jinny Blom); 178–179 Clive Nichols/GPL /Photolibrary (Designer: Stephen Woodhams); 180 Chris Tubbs/Red Cover; 180–181 Alessandra Santarelli (Architect: Ian Hay); 181 Mel Yates/Media10 Syndication (Architect: Project Orange); 182-183 Mads Mogensen (Architect: Peter Wenger); 184 above Richard Sprengler /Rocio Romero; 184 below Richard Sprengler/Rocio Romero; 184–185 above Stellan Herner; 184–185 below W. Waldron /Photozest; 186 Vincent Leroux/Marie Claire Maison (Stylist: Josée Postic); 186–187 Ivan Terestchenko /Maison Madame Figaro/Camera Press; 187 John Dummer /Taverne Agency (Stylist: Fransien Schut); 190–193 Undine Prohl (Architect: Dry Design); 194–197 Chris Tubbs/Conran Octopus (Architect: Adam Richards); 198–201 Christian Sarramon (Architect: Jean-Louis Menard); 202–205 Elizabeth Felicella (Architect: Messana O'Rorke Architects); 206–209 Chris Tubbs/Conran Octopus (Architect: Woollacott Gilmartin Architects); 210–213 Katsuhisa Kida (Architects: Takaharu + Yui Tezuka/Tezuka Architects, Masahiro Ikeda/Masahiro Ikeda co., ltd)(Lighting design: Masahide Kakudate/Masahide Kakudate Lighting Architect & Associates); 224 Richard Powers (Architect: LOH Architects)

Every effort has been made to trace the copyright holders. We apologize in advance for any unintentional omissions and would be pleased to insert the appropriate acknowledgment in any subsequent publication.